Julie Stafford's
SALADS

GW00801672

VIKING

Viking
Penguin Books Australia Ltd
487 Maroondah Highway, PO Box 257
Ringwood, Victoria 3134, Australia
Penguin Books Ltd
Harmondsworth, Middlesex, England
Penguin Putnam Inc.
375 Hudson Street, New York, New York 10014, USA
Penguin Books Canada Limited
10 Alcorn Avenue, Toronto, Ontario, Canada M4V 3B2
Penguin Books (NZ) Ltd
Cnr Rosedale and Airborne Roads, Albany, Auckland, New Zealand
Penguin Books (South Africa) (Pty) Limited
4 Pallinghurst Road, Parktown 2193, South Africa

First published by Penguin Books Australia Ltd, 1998

10 9 8 7 6 5 4 3

Design by Glenn Thomas, Penguin Design Studio
Photography by Mark Chew
Food preparation and styling by Deborah McLean
Illustrations by Michelle Ryan and Cathy Larsen
Typeset in 11/14 pt Officina Sans by Post Pre-press Group, Brisbane, Queensland
Printed and bound in Australia by Australian Print Group, Maryborough, Victoria

National Library of Australia
Cataloguing-in-Publication data

Stafford, Julie.
 Julie Stafford's salads.

 Includes index.
 ISBN 0 670 86770 5.

 1. Salads. I. Title. II. Title: Salads.

641.83

*Front cover photograph: Grapefruit, Mango, Avocado and Greens with Ginger
Vinaigrette (see page 62), with chargrilled chicken fillet.*

Contents

Acknowledgements

As always, thank you to the great team at Penguin Australia who enable me to take my simple food philosophy to the marketplace in such an easy-to-use, fun format.

Special thanks must also go to those caring fruit, vegetable and herb growers who understand the true value and purpose of plant foods in the life-cycle of human beings. They lovingly go about tilling and nurturing their soils to grow crops of chemically uncontaminated produce, which they deliver to the marketplace so that all of us can enjoy their nutritional value and natural taste.

Introduction

It is summer time, Christmas is just around the corner, the annual beach holiday beckons, and my friends at Penguin have set me the task of gathering my favourite salad recipes for another title in the *Taste of Life* series.

Salads are not just my favourite foods, they really are the life-force of our diet. Fresh vegetables, fruits, herbs and spices are all rich in antioxidants and essential nutrients that assist in our survival, the day-to-day function of our organs, and disease prevention. Not only are they incredibly good for us, they also taste sensational.

Those of us seeking optimum health are no longer prepared to accept just a simple salad of lettuce, tomato and cucumber or munch on an apple and banana to get our daily quota of these fabulous foods. We recognise that good health is the synergistic combination of many essential factors from a wide variety of sources. Salads created from fresh fruits, vegetables or a combination of both, with pasta, rice, nuts, seeds, dried fruits, seafood and lean meats, and enhanced in flavour with the addition of herbs, spices and dressings made from good-quality oils and vinegars, are not just a meal, they are a dynamic, health-giving package of vitality and energy.

The health status of the Mediterranean peoples has taught us in recent years that not all fats are bad for us. Although we need both saturated and unsaturated fats in our diet to be physically and mentally healthy, the ideal diet is one that cuts back on the saturated fats found in butter, margarine, full-cream milk, yoghurt, ice-cream, eggs, fish, poultry and meat, and encourages the use of acceptable amounts of unsaturated fats found in vegetable oils like sunflower, sesame, safflower, corn and flaxseed oils, nuts like walnuts, hazelnuts and brazils, and monounsaturated fats, especially those in olive and canola oils, seeds and avocados, and nuts like peanuts, cashews and almonds. But remember that the fat in these foods comes in a concentrated form, and we only need a small amount for their health value.

Let's begin!

First, a quick call to Melrose Health Supplies for a shipment of their best organic oils, vinegars, tahini, plus the essential flagon of apple juice concentrate (a sugar substitute used in all the *Taste of Life* cookbooks), and their fabulous new cholesterol and egg-free mayonnaise – a must-have! I particularly like the Melrose oils because they are bottled in dark-coloured glass, which protects the oil from exposure to light and therefore oxidation.

Next is a stop at the fruit and vegetable shop for the best fresh ingredients and herbs. I gather as much home-grown produce as possible. There is something special about a salad made from ingredients 'fresh from the vine'.

The butcher knows me well enough by now to give me his best lean beef, lamb and chicken fillets. These food items are costly enough without paying for fat and skin that simply gets discarded.

Lastly, a visit to the supermarket and the local deli to stock up on pasta, rice, essential canned items like chickpeas, beans, tuna, corn kernels, salt-free tomato juice, spices, mustards, my favourite sweet chilli sauce, a large bottle of low-salt soy sauce and a jar of pesto.

Orange, Cucumber and Mint Salad. A hearty Potato Salad with Mustard Mayo Dressing. Assorted Salad Greens with Balsamic Dressing. Roasted Roma Tomato and Thyme Salad. Snow Pea, Mango and Avocado Salad with Pesto Dressing. These salads have been part of our Christmas table alongside the array of cold meats and fish for as long as I can remember, and they never fail to rekindle memories of wonderful family gatherings. No-one can imagine not serving these salads on Christmas Day!

Our salads usually take advantage of the wonderful variety of seasonal vegetables and fruits available to us throughout the year. Popular salads during summer include asparagus with a simple vinaigrette and Beetroot in a Honey, Soy and Sesame Dressing. Spicy Chargrilled Mushroom Salad is Dad's favourite, and ideal with barbecued meats. Our Tomato, Onion and Basil Salad is made with real tomatoes, like those Dad remembers from years ago, 'when tomatoes were red, not pink, and tasted like tomatoes should'. One or two salads are designed to be complete meals all on their own, like the Sweet Potato and Chickpea Salad with Chilli Tahini Dressing or the Tomato and Mushroom Pasta Salad with Red Pepper Mayo Dressing. Many recipes in this book will satisfy the vegetarians in the family or those of us who want to have a meat-free day after the excesses of Christmas, or any other celebration.

For me, holidays at the beach are about family and friends, relaxation, and a time to research food trends, new ingredients and new ideas that match my simple food philosophy that food should not only taste good, but be good for you. Taste-testing at the beach is now an expectation, and always lots of fun. There are plenty of mouths to feed and lots of opinions. On one occasion, the local Federal Member popped in and was amazed to see so many ingredients going into a salad dressing. 'This looks like a political nightmare. Surely it's easier to buy a jar of salad dressing at the local supermarket,' he suggested. It probably is, but I still haven't found one that provides the taste without the fat.

It is also far more economical to have a range of good-quality oils and vinegars on hand and a variety of herbs and spices so you can dress a salad to match the flavours and textures of the ingredients used. Sometimes a dressing might be just a mix of a few ingredients, allowing the salad ingredients to star. At other times a dressing might be a marriage of several ingredients that provides a richness, a piquancy or a creamy smooth texture that gives a surprise with every mouthful.

A holiday-maker asked if we needed another salad book. 'After all, isn't the best salad just a mixture of what's in the bottom of the refrigerator with a dash of oil, vinegar and whatever herb you can find in the garden?' This comes from a friend whom I suspect goes to the garden, collects a bunch of flowers, plonks them in a vase, and creates a stunning arrangement every time. But such confidence in the kitchen does not come naturally to everyone.

This book is designed to help you build such a confidence by introducing you to perhaps new salad ingredients and especially new combinations of salad ingredients. I hope it encourages you to explore some simple, fun and tasty dressing ideas, using ingredients you may not normally keep at the bottom of the refrigerator or in your pantry.

Good health and good salad making!

Julie Stafford

Glossary of Ingredients

apple juice concentrate
A syrup–sugar substitute used in the *Taste of Life* cookbooks to provide sweetness in recipes, but with much fewer kilojoules than refined sugar or honey. (It is apple juice boiled down to a syrup and can be reconstituted to a juice drink by adding water.)

balsamic vinegar
A vinegar made from unfermented Trebbiano grapes grown in the foothills of Modena, Italy. Its unique dark red-rust colour livens salads when used alone or with a good olive oil. Its rich flavour is the result of its age, the quality of the original wine, and the type of wood the storage barrel is made of.

basil
A member of the mint family, with aromatic, sweet, liquorice-scented leaves. The foliage is either green or purple, and a perfect complement to tomatoes, chicken, fish and other salad greens. Chopped, it adds a delicious flavour to a vinaigrette. For a fabulous creamy mayonnaise-style pesto, blend some fresh leaves with yoghurt, pinenuts and a little parmesan cheese.

capers
The small unopened flowerbuds of the caper bush. They usually come pickled in white vinegar and are sold in jars. Add to a vinaigrette for a strong, aromatic flavour, or add a few to a finished salad or coleslaw.

chillies (fresh)
The red ones are generally hotter than the green, and the smaller the chilli, the hotter the taste! I mostly use the red ones, as you only need a little to get the best taste. Diced, they add an interesting red colour and texture to a dressing. Beware of the seeds and membrane, where the majority of the heat lies. Remove before dicing and, if possible, work with gloves.

chives

A member of the onion family, but the taste is very mild. The fine, green, grass-like foliage adds flavour and texture to potato, bean, rice and vegetable salads, and the traditional coleslaw.

cider vinegar

A vinegar made from fermenting apples. It has a sharp flavour due to its high acid content. Be careful not to overuse, especially with salad ingredients that have their own strong flavours. I like it mainly on salads that contain fruits like pear and apple.

coconut milk

Canned coconut milk is thinner than coconut cream and lower in fat. It can be further diluted with water or skim milk. To make your own coconut milk, blend $1/2$ cup warm milk with 1 tablespoon shredded coconut and strain.

coriander

A common herb in Thai cooking. Coriander has delicate, wispy, pale green foliage that adds a distinctively Oriental flavour to salads, but a little goes a long way. It enhances the flavour of a sesame or peanut oil dressing, and goes well with chicken, beef, fish and fruits, especially oranges, pears and apples. It works well in an oil-free vinaigrette that uses fresh orange juice as a base.

corn kernels

Corn is a good fibre food and tasty addition to the salad bowl. Keep a couple of cans (salt-free) in your pantry to add to potato, chickpea and bean, and vegetable salads, and coleslaw.

couscous

Small pellets made by rubbing semolina grains into white flour, which is then cooked and dried.

crabmeat

Once again, look for low-salt varieties or rinse well-drained crabmeat under cold running water to remove excess salt. It is higher in cholesterol than most fish and should be used sparingly. The best brands are expensive, but they taste sweeter and you only need to add a little to a salad of other ingredients to enjoy it.

cracked wheat
Whole grain that has cracked or broken in the early stages of milling. It is the traditional base for Tabbouleh Salad, although you can substitute rice or couscous.

cumin
A warm aromatic spice often used in curry-style recipes. It works well in yoghurt and citrus-based dressings.

curry paste
Of the prepared curry pastes available I particularly like the hot vindaloo variety – a little makes a big impact. The flavour of curry paste is much more intense than curry powder. For every tablespoon of curry powder, use only about 1 teaspoon of paste.

curry powder
There are several blends available, but they are mostly composed of varying amounts of the following ground herbs and spices: coriander, turmeric, chilli, cumin, fennel, fenugreek, mustard, ginger, cinnamon, nutmeg and cloves. You can use a commercial mix or make up your own.

dill
Has very fine, feathery foliage and a slightly aniseed taste that goes well with salads of fish, potatoes, cucumber, most other vegetables, and adds an interesting dimension to coleslaw.

dried fruits
Not everybody likes the sweetness of dried fruits in their salad, so it pays to check. You can soak the fruits in a little warm water before adding them to the salad or leave them as they are if you like their chewy texture. Marinating them in a vinaigrette (not creamy-style dressings) will allow them to absorb the flavours of

the dressing. The best fruits to use are sultanas, raisins, currants, dates and apricots.

fish sauce
A sauce made from fermenting anchovies. It is traditionally used to flavour Thai and Vietnamese dishes. There are low-salt varieties available.

five-spice powder
A pungent spice made up of cinnamon, cloves, fennel, star anise and Sichuan peppercorns.

garlic
A peeled garlic clove added to a vinaigrette gives a very subtle garlic flavour. Chopped garlic imparts a slightly stronger garlic flavour, and crushed garlic cloves offer the most intense garlic flavour of all.

ginger
You'll find these knobbly roots at the supermarket or greengrocer. Look for young ones with taut, thin skin (they are less fibrous and have more juice). Peel before using and finely dice or place small pieces in a garlic press to crush. Ginger is prized for its sweet and slightly spicy flavour.

ginger, pickled
At the very best food stores you'll find small jars of thin shavings of ginger, which have been pickled in a solution of sugar and vinegar. The flavour is sensational, and you only need the smallest amount to enhance whatever you're adding it to.

herbs
These not only add that burst of exciting flavour to a salad, they are a rich source of micro-nutrients. To enjoy the best taste and health properties, herbs should be used as fresh as possible. Try growing some at home. They grow well anywhere in the garden and in pots, as long as there is plenty of sunshine. Use both the

leaves and stems, chopped up and scattered over salads or added to dressings for extra flavour. The amount given in each recipe is merely a guideline and depends on your taste. Fresh herbs can be replaced with the dried: about 1 teaspoon of dried herb is equivalent to 1 tablespoon of chopped fresh herb, but the flavour is quite different. I like to keep dried herbs for recipes that have long cooking times. See also alphabetical listings.

honey
An essential ingredient in dressings that use curry, soy and tahini, where it adds sweetness, but particularly for its unique ability to complement these ingredients. Warm slightly before adding to other dressing ingredients for a perfect smooth result.

juices
Freshly squeezed are definitely the best. Lemon, lime and orange juices are most often used in dressings, but you can also use apple, pear, pineapple, tomato, carrot or a combination.

mayonnaise
Choose low-fat, cholesterol-free commercial mayonnaise. My preferred choice is a cholesterol and egg-free mayonnaise made by Melrose Health Supplies. I also give two recipes for mayonnaise, one creamy and the other dairy-free, in the dressings chapter.

mint
Mostly recognised for its refreshing, tangy taste, mint adds a distinctive flavour to a vinaigrette and is excellent in salads like tomato, onion and mint, and orange, cucumber and mint. Or add a few leaves to a Salad of Greens and especially to fruit salads. This is a herb best grown in a pot, to contain its root system.

mirin
Mainly used in Japanese or Chinese recipes but often used as a white wine substitute in mild-flavoured salad dressings. It is made from fermented rice and its neutral colour is ideal when a dressing is designed to be subtle and not the star attraction.

mustard, Dijon
A smooth, sharp, but not too hot tasting, creamy mustard paste.

mustard, dry
Finely ground mustard seeds.

mustard, English
A smooth, very hot mustard paste.

mustard, grain
Black and brown mustard seeds in a creamy mustard paste with a strong, pungent taste. Flavours vary depending on the quantity and quality of vinegar or wine used in the recipe.

mustard seeds
The black, brown or yellow seeds can be added to a vinaigrette to add extra spice and texture. Homemade herb vinegars use the whole seed with other herbs as the flavour is more subtle and develops from mild to hot the longer the vinegars stand.

nuts
A high-energy food containing about 80 per cent monounsaturated fats (like the fats in olive oil). Nuts also add nourishment, flavour and an interesting crunchy texture to salads. Nutritionally, they tend to be a good source of protein, potassium, magnesium, some zinc and iron. Almonds and pistachios are an excellent source of calcium. They can be added whole or chopped, raw or dry-roasted. Break the nuts between your fingers to release the natural oils. I have mainly used peanuts, cashews, pecans, pistachios, pinenuts and walnuts, but you can also use brazil, almond, hazelnut and macadamia nuts. Nuts are best used fresh. Buy them still in their shells and shell as you need them. Store in a dark, cool, dry place and keep for no longer than 6 weeks. Because of their high fat content, nuts turn rancid quite quickly, so buy in small amounts.

oils

Use oils that are first pressed (virgin), often obtained by hand-pressing, and stored in dark bottles. Always taste oil before you use it. It should be good enough to drink and its unique flavour obvious. If it looks cloudy or tastes bitter, discard as it is most probably rancid. I have mainly used safflower, olive, peanut, hazelnut and sesame oils in this book, but you can use mustard, almond, grapeseed, corn, pecan, sunflower, walnut or a blend of vegetable oils. You'll find a wide array of flavoured oils at speciality supermarkets and delis. Be careful when buying these as quite often they are made from cheap refined oils with the addition of garlic, sesame seeds, chillies and herbs. See also alphabetical listings.

olive oil

A staple ingredient of the Mediterranean diet, obtained by pressing the ripe pulp of the olives after picking. The fat is predominantly monounsaturated. Use a small amount as the base of a salad dressing to enjoy the oil's nutritional benefits. This is much healthier than cooking with the oil because temperatures that are too high can actually change the structure of the fatty acids, making it rancid and harmful to your health.

olives

These small fruits are high in monounsaturated fats, and much prized for their sharp and fruity taste. They are often salty because of the curing process. Use a small amount for flavour instead of building a salad around them. Both green (immature) olives and black (mature) olives can be used for salads. They often come flavoured with garlic cloves, chillies and herbs.

parsley

With its rich green colour and mild flavour, parsley is one of those herbs that can be added to practically any salad. It is extremely compatible with other herbs. Choose from the curly-leafed or the flat-leafed Italian variety.

pasta

Keep a good supply of (egg-free) pasta on hand. It makes an excellent salad base to which you can add a variety of cooked vegetables, meats and herbs and salad dressings. Explore all the different-shaped pasta available to bring fun to the pasta salad.

peanut oil

An oil with a distinctive peanut flavour, where a little goes a long way. The fat is of a monounsaturated nature.

pepper

Finely ground black pepper is mostly used in salad dressings and freshly ground black pepper is usually used to give added flavour to the whole salad. You can substitute white pepper in salad dressings for a more subtle flavour or if you don't want tiny black specks all over your ingredients. I personally like the bite of black pepper. You might also like to try a Cajun-style pepper.

pesto

While a variety of commercial pesto sauces are available, there is nothing quite like fresh, homemade pesto. Although the quantities of ingredients can change, the ingredients are always the same: fresh basil leaves, pinenuts, garlic, romano or parmesan cheese, and a good olive oil. Blend the first ingredients together and add enough oil to achieve a paste-like consistency.

pulses

Dried beans, peas and lentils are high in vegetable protein and rich in amino acids. They contain iron but for maximum absorption, should be consumed with other fruits and vegetables containing vitamin C. Pulses can feature as a base for a salad, or put some into a salad to add interest and lift the nutritional value of the salad. Not all pulses are ideal for use in salads. Chickpeas, lentils, red kidney beans, broad beans, lima beans, borlotti beans and cannellini beans are ideal.

red wine vinegar

As the name implies, this is a vinegar made from red wine, so its flavour is dependent on the original wine and the storage barrels. It is particularly good with stone fruit, and provides a wonderful sauce when added to the pan juices of cooked meat. The sauce is then cooled, and becomes the basis of a dressing to serve over meats like lamb and beef.

rice

Includes brown rice, which has three times more fibre than white rice, basmati and Arborio (short-grain Italian) rice.

rosemary

This shrub has very fine, pine-like needles that are strong and very aromatic. You only need a small amount. I like to throw it over oven-baked or roasted vegetables for a milder flavour and a wonderful warmth. It is also a good herb for flavouring vinegars to be added to salads. Simply place sprigs of rosemary in a bottle and pour over warm vinegar. Seal and store the herb vinegar for at least a week before using.

safflower oil

Safflower oil is regarded as the 'king' of polyunsaturated oils because of its rich source of polyunsaturated oilseed. Its rather bland taste makes it an ideal oil for salads containing ingredients that have assertive flavours of their own.

salt

Some recipes and dressings call for a pinch of salt. A small pinch is about $1/8$ teaspoon and a large pinch is about $1/4$ teaspoon. Salt can enhance and sharpen the flavour of a lot of ingredients, particularly tomatoes, but be careful not to overuse. Aim to cut back, don't use it at every mealtime, and use herbs to experience a wide range of flavours. Much of the salt in our diet tends to come in a hidden form, from canned, processed, take-away and cured foods.

seeds

These have the same nutritional value as nuts. Scatter them over your salads to add another dimension. Sesame seeds, pumpkin seeds, poppyseeds and sunflower seeds are often used in salads.

sesame oil

An oil used in salad recipes specifically for its unique nutty flavour. You'll often find it teamed with other ingredients like fresh ginger, soy sauce, chilli and honey. The fat in sesame oil is predominantly an even mix of polyunsaturated and mono-unsaturated.

soy sauce

A dark, thin sauce made from fermented soy beans. Use only the low-salt variety.

sun-dried tomatoes

Naturally sun-dried tomatoes that are marinated in olive oil. They are high in salt. To enjoy their flavour, you only need a small amount. Drain oil from tomatoes before using and place them on paper towels to absorb any remaining oil.

sweet chilli sauce

This is a must-have condiment if you like chillies. There are different varieties available, so choose one that is low in salt and sugar. You only need the tiniest amount to enjoy its delicious taste.

tahini

A creamy paste made by grinding sesame seeds. There are two varieties, hulled and unhulled. I have used the hulled (where the outside husk of the sesame seed is removed before grinding) mainly for its lighter texture and taste. Tahini is high in protein and calcium. It can be added to yoghurt to make a creamy mayonnaise-style dressing or to vinegar and orange juice to make a vinaigrette-style dressing. It has a unique peanut taste and is a highly regarded food in a vegetarian diet.

tandoori paste

A blend of very fragrant and spicy Indian spices like paprika, cumin, turmeric, chilli, coriander, tamarind, ginger, cardamom, saffron, and garam masala in a paste. It is mainly used on meats as a marinade to add flavour before baking, grilling or barbecuing.

thyme

Both the foliage and flowers from the shrub can be used to flavour vegetables and meats. I particularly like thyme with a salad of tomatoes, roasted capsicums, zucchini and chicken.

tuna

Look for tuna in springwater (low-salt). Canned tuna has the same nutritional value as fresh tuna and is very convenient if you need to whip up a quick meal. Tuna is a low-cholesterol fish.

vindaloo curry paste

For me, another must-have condiment. It provides just the right mix of herbs and spices and you need only a little to experience wonderful curry-flavoured dressings or salads.

vinegars

Like oils, there are a lot choose from. You don't use much in salad dressings, so this is one ingredient worth spending more on. Look for a good-quality white and mild red vinegar, a balsamic vinegar and a cider vinegar for extra sharpness. Unlike oils, they add little nutritional value. See also alphabetical listings.

white wine vinegar

A delicately flavoured vinegar made from white wine. Like red wine vinegar, its flavour depends on the original wine it is made from. It is an ideal vinegar to use as a base for making your own herb, garlic, chilli and raspberry vinegars. Heat the vinegar and pour over your favourite flavouring ingredients that you have packed into a bottle. For the best flavours, allow them to stand for as long as possible. Sometimes the flavour of a homemade vinegar (without the addition of oil) is all a salad requires.

yoghurt

Use a plain, bland, not too bitter, low-fat variety of not more than 1 per cent fat content yoghurt. If you need to avoid dairy foods, substitute soy yoghurt or soymilk in recipes that call for yoghurt or milk.

Glossary of Terms

al dente
A term usually used for cooking pasta and rice but also used for vegetables. It means to cook food until just tender, yet still retaining a little bite.

blanch
To plunge raw food (usually vegetables) in boiling water until cooked, then remove. Refresh immediately by plunging them into iced water for a few minutes to cool completely, then drain. Alternatively vegetables can be steam-blanched in the microwave. Blanching enhances the vegetable colour, removes bitter tastes, loosens the skin of some fruits and vegetables, and the vegetables themselves retain a lovely crispness.

bruise
To partially crush foods like garlic, ginger, peppercorns or nuts. Bruising can be done between the fingers, with the blade of a large knife or with a mortar and pestle.

chargrill
To cook vegetables, meat and fish over a hot grill pan that is specially designed for chargrilling. Chargrilling will leave your food with scorch lines. If the pan is very hot before you place food on it, there should be no need to add any oil. The very hot surface will seal the food quickly, allowing no juices to escape. (It is the juices lost during the cooking process that act like a glue between the food and the surface.)

chop
To cut food roughly into no particular shape or size. Use your own discretion.

devein
To remove the black intestinal vein of prawns.

dice
The process of chopping fruits and vegetables into small, even cubes.

dry-roast
To cook food by dry heat either under the griller, in the oven or in a non-stick pan over an open flame.

fillet
A piece of meat or fish that has no bones, with all fat and skin removed.

julienne
To cut fruit or vegetables (e.g. apple, zucchini, carrot) into very thin matchstick strips.

marinate
To cover foods with a combination of wet or dry ingredients and allowing them to stand for at least an hour to absorb the flavours of the marinade and promote a more intense flavour.

pinch
Usually refers to a small amount of salt, pepper, dried herbs or spices that can be held between two fingertips.

poach
To cook fruit, vegetables, chicken or fish in simmering liquid (water, wine, stock, juice).

prepare salad greens
To remove stems, root or core of salad vegetables, discarding any yellow, wilted or bruised leaves. Cover leaves with lots of cold water and gently move the lettuce around in the water with your hands to allow grit to sink to the bottom of the washing vessel. Lift leaves gently and drain in a colander. Over-handling of the leaves at this stage will cause bruising. Transfer leaves to a salad spinner or rest on layers of paper towels or gently wrap in tea

towels to absorb excess moisture. Leaves should always be as dry as possible before you add other ingredients, especially the dressing.

purée
To blend fruits, vegetables or dressing ingredients until a smooth texture is achieved.

rest
To set cooked meats aside after cooking to allow the meat tissue to relax and reabsorb the cooking juices, which results in more tender and juicy meat.

segment
To break or cut up fruit such as orange and grapefruit into individual wedges. Completely remove peel and visible pith from citrus fruits before slicing.

simmer
To cook food in liquid which is just bubbling.

steam
To cook food with steam in a pan. The food is placed on a rack above boiling liquid, and the steam penetrates and cooks the food without it coming into contact with water. Food can also be steam-cooked in a microwave oven.

whisk
To beat in a continuous motion with a wire whisk until the mixture is well blended.

With such an abundance and wide variety of ingredients available these days, **salads** don't have to end with summer. Whether you choose to eat them as a complete meal or as a complement to other foods, the rules are the same. Choose the freshest and best-looking ingredients available and present them in a way that is appealing to both the eye and the palate. You can slice, shred, chop, dice, grate or julienne to vary the taste and texture of a salad. Always prepare a salad close to eating time, and keep the combinations simple so that the subtle flavours of each ingredient can be savoured with the dressing.

Apple, Celery and Walnut Coleslaw

SERVES 4–6

Walnuts are moderately high in protein and are a rich source of polyunsaturated fats. Their strong, buttery, distinctive flavour combines well with apple and makes this coleslaw a meal in itself.

$^1/_2$ cup Creamy Mayonnaise (page 130)
$^1/_2$ small cabbage, thinly sliced
2 red apples, cored and thinly sliced or diced
2 Granny Smith apples, cored and thinly sliced or diced
2 sticks celery, finely sliced
1 red onion, peeled, thinly sliced or diced or $^1/_2$ cup finely chopped
    spring onions
100 g walnuts, finely chopped
1 tablespoon finely grated lemon zest

- Make the dressing as instructed and set aside.
- To make salad, place all ingredients in a bowl and add dressing. Toss lightly and serve.

Serve with chicken, turkey, lamb, beef or chargrilled vegetables.

Apple, Corn and Pineapple Coleslaw

SERVES 4–6

Use white or Savoy cabbage for this salad. White cabbage has pale greenish-white, tightly furled leaves. The Savoy has darkish-green crinkly leaves and a slightly milder flavour. Choose a cabbage that makes a snapping noise when the leaves are broken. This suggests it is fresh and full of flavour. Store in a sealed plastic bag or container at the bottom of your refrigerator until required. Wash thoroughly after slicing, as dirt, insects and sometimes grubs tend to gather between the leaves. I like to shred cabbage for coleslaw in a food processor to give a very thin and even texture. If using a knife, discard any coarse stems and leaves.

$1/2$ cup Creamy Mayonnaise (page 130)
$1/2$ small cabbage, thinly sliced
1×420 g can salt-free corn kernels, well drained or 250 g cold, cooked corn kernels
1×440 g can crushed pineapple in natural juice, well drained or 300 g fresh pineapple, finely chopped
1 small red capsicum, seeded and chopped
5 spring onions, finely chopped or $1/2$ salad onion, peeled and diced, plus $1/2$ cup finely chopped chives
$1/8$–$1/4$ teaspoon cayenne pepper

- Make the dressing as instructed and set aside.
- To make salad, place all ingredients in a bowl and add dressing and pepper to taste. Toss lightly and serve.

Serve with fish, chicken, lamb, beef, chargrilled vegetables or baked potatoes.

Apple, Pear and Pecan Salad

SERVES 4–6

You don't always need a lot of ingredients to make a great-tasting salad, but you do need great-tasting ones. Make sure the apples and pears are slightly chilled, and firm with no bruises. Use different varieties of pears and apples to change the flavour of the salad. I like hard, crisp Bartlett pears with Lady William or Fuji apples. When adding pecans to your salad, break them up between your fingers to release the pecan oils.

dressing
2 tablespoons freshly squeezed lemon juice
2 teaspoons red wine vinegar
1 tablespoon olive oil

3–4 apples, cored and thinly sliced
3–4 pears, cored and thinly sliced
1/2 cup pecans, broken up

- To make dressing, place all ingredients except the oil in a jar and shake well. Pour into a small bowl and slowly whisk in the oil.
- To make salad, place all ingredients in a bowl or on a platter and add dressing. Toss lightly and serve.

Serve with salad greens, fish, chicken or turkey.

Asparagus and Greens with Pistachios and Balsamic Vinaigrette

SERVES 4–6

This is a refreshing, tangy, tasty salad that works well as a starter. Not only does it taste great, but the pistachios are high in iron and protein. Who said healthy food had to be boring food!

2 tablespoons Balsamic Vinaigrette (page 128)
200 g mixed salad greens
800 g asparagus spears, stems removed
50 g dry-roasted pistachios, chopped

- Make the dressing as instructed and set aside.
- Prepare greens as for Salad of Greens (page 97).
- Blanch the asparagus.
- To make salad, combine all ingredients and add dressing. Toss lightly and serve. Alternatively, you may like to serve the salad on individual plates. Divide salad greens and asparagus spears evenly among plates, scatter over the pistachios and spoon over a little dressing.

Serve with chargrilled vegetables, fish or chicken.

Asparagus and Snow Pea Salad with Honey, Soy and Sesame Dressing

SERVES 4–6

Simple salads are sometimes the best salads!

1/4 cup Honey, Soy and Sesame Dressing (page 135)
600 g asparagus spears, stems removed and spears cut into julienne
600 g snow peas, topped, tailed and cut into julienne
1 teaspoon sesame seeds (optional)

- Make the dressing as instructed and set aside.
- Blanch the vegetables.
- To make salad, combine all ingredients and add dressing. Toss lightly, garnish with sesame seeds and serve.

Serve with fish, chicken, beef, lamb, Salad of Greens (page 97) or chargrilled vegetables.

Asparagus, Feta and Walnut Salad

SERVES 4-6

The sharp taste of feta combined with a lemony dressing and crunchy roasted walnuts make this a delightful way to serve asparagus. Try it as an entrée. The remaining asparagus stems make a great soup.

dressing
2 tablespoons freshly squeezed lemon juice
2 teaspoons red or white wine vinegar
1 tablespoon olive, canola or walnut oil

200 g low-fat feta
1.5 kg large asparagus spears, blanched
$1/2$ cup walnuts, broken into small pieces

- To make dressing, place all ingredients except the oil in a jar and shake well. Pour into a small bowl and slowly whisk in the oil.
- Crumble feta to about large breadcrumb size or cut into small cubes.
- To make salad, combine all ingredients and add dressing. Toss lightly, taking care not to break up the feta too much, and serve. Alternatively, you may like to serve the asparagus on individual plates. Divide feta and walnuts evenly among plates and spoon over a little dressing.

Serve with fish, chicken, turkey, tomatoes, chargrilled vegetables or Salad of Greens (page 97).

Avocado, Mango and Orange with Butter Lettuce and Chilli Dressing

SERVES 4–6

The soft, delicate and subtle yet buttery lettuce allows the mango, avocado and orange to take centre stage here. The recipe also works well with peppery watercress. I suggest you try both.

dressing

2 teaspoons freshly squeezed lemon juice

2 teaspoons freshly squeezed orange juice

1 teaspoon cider vinegar

1 teaspoon sweet chilli sauce (page 10)

1 tablespoon safflower oil

1 large head butter lettuce

1 large, ripe, firm mango

1 large, ripe, firm avocado

4 navel oranges

- To make dressing, place all ingredients except the oil in a jar and shake well. Pour into a small bowl and slowly whisk in the oil.
- Remove the core of the lettuce and prepare leaves as for salad greens.
- Peel mango and cut into thin slices.
- Peel avocado and cut into thin slices.
- Peel oranges and cut into thin rounds.
- To make salad, combine all ingredients and add dressing. Toss lightly, taking care not to bruise the avocado and mango, and serve.

Serve with fish, chicken or turkey.

Avocado, Tomato and Carrot Salad

SERVES 4–6

You can change the nature of this salad just by varying the size of the cut vegetables. A very small diced version of the salad is almost like a salsa and can be served more as a sauce than as a salad.

2 tablespoons Vinaigrette (page 146)
2 avocados, peeled and diced
4 tomatoes, seeded and diced
2 carrots, diced
1 red onion, peeled and diced
$1/4$ cup olives, pitted and finely chopped
1 cup finely chopped parsley
freshly ground black pepper

- Make the dressing as instructed and set aside.
- To make salad, combine all ingredients and add the dressing and pepper to taste. Toss lightly and serve.

Serve with chargrilled vegetables, lamb, beef, chicken, fish, boiled potatoes, beetroot, baked potato or Salad of Greens (page 97).

Bean Sprouts, Sugar Peas and Avocado with Balsamic Vinaigrette

SERVES 4–6

One of my favourite lunches is a warm crusty wholemeal or wholegrain roll filled with lots of salad greens and this salad. It is also perfect wrapped up in a fresh pita round.

dressing
2 tablespoons Balsamic Vinaigrette (page 128)
a pinch of salt
a pinch of pepper

200 g bean sprouts
150 g sugar peas, topped and tailed
1 large, ripe avocado, peeled and diced
1/2 red capsicum, seeded and diced
2 Roma tomatoes, seeded and diced
1 medium zucchini, ends removed, halved and cut into julienne
1/2 cup basil leaves
1/4 cup mint leaves

- Make the dressing as instructed, adding salt and pepper to taste. Set aside.
- Wash and drain bean sprouts.
- Blanch sugar peas.
- Combine avocado, capsicum and tomato.
- To make salad, combine bean sprouts, peas, zucchini, basil and mint. Top with combined avocado, capsicum and tomato. Add dressing, toss lightly and serve.

Serve with beef, lamb, chicken, fish or chargrilled vegetables.

Beef and Mushroom Salad with Balsamic Vinaigrette

SERVES 4–6

Chargrilling the mushrooms gives them a slightly smoky flavour that goes very well with the balsamic vinegar.

2 tablespoons Balsamic Vinaigrette (page 128)
500–800 g lean beef
1 tablespoon crushed garlic
1 tablespoon finely grated orange zest
1 tablespoon grainy mustard
400 g cultivated or field mushrooms
250 g lettuce greens
1–2 tablespoons finely chopped chervil, marjoram or chives

- Make the dressing as instructed and set aside.
- Marinate beef in garlic, orange zest and mustard for at least 2 hours.
- Chargrill beef on both sides until brown but still a little pink on the inside. (Depending on the thickness, the meat only needs a couple of minutes on each side if you like it rare.) Leave the beef to rest before slicing thinly and save any cooked meat juices to add to the dressing.
- Grill mushrooms in a chargrill pan or cook them under the griller.
- To make salad, combine all ingredients and add dressing. Toss lightly and serve.

Serve with chargrilled vegetables.

Beef, Carrot and Caper Salad

SERVES 4-6

Most people either love or hate capers. I love the sharp taste of these pickled unopened flowerbuds of the caper bush. Try one or two capers before you try it in the salad.

2 tablespoons Vinaigrette (page 146)
500–800 g lean beef
1 tablespoon crushed garlic
1 tablespoon finely grated orange zest
200 g lettuce greens
250 g carrot, julienned
$1/2$ cup capers
$1/4$ cup finely chopped parsley or chives

- Make the dressing as instructed and set aside.
- Combine beef with the garlic and orange zest for at least 2 hours before cooking.
- Chargrill beef on both sides until brown but still a little pink on the inside. (Depending on the thickness, the meat only needs a couple of minutes on each side if you like it rare.) Leave the beef to rest before slicing thinly and save any cooked meat juices to add to the dressing.
- Prepare greens as for Salad of Greens (page 97).
- To make salad, scatter lettuce greens over the base of a salad platter. Top with beef, then carrot, followed by capers, parsley or chives and spoon over the dressing.

Serve with chargrilled vegetables, rice or pasta.

Beef, Spinach and Beans Salad with Thai Dressing

SERVES 4–6

For succulent tender beef every time, use the best quality beef you can find and cook it in a very hot pan, turning the meat only once during cooking. Brown the outside to seal in the juices and vary the cooking time according to how well done you want the inside to be. Prime beef can be served very pink.

1/4 cup Thai Dressing (page 144)
500–800 g lean beef
2 cloves garlic, peeled and crushed
2 teaspoons finely chopped fresh ginger
200 g baby spinach leaves, washed
250 g green beans, topped, tailed, cut into four and blanched
250 g yellow beans, topped, tailed, cut into four and blanched
1 tablespoon sesame seeds

- Make the dressing as instructed and set aside.
- Combine the beef and the garlic and ginger for at least 2 hours before cooking.
- Chargrill beef on both sides until brown but still a little pink on the inside. (Depending on the thickness, the meat only needs a couple of minutes on each side if you like it rare.) Leave the beef to rest before slicing thinly and save any cooked meat juices to add to the dressing.
- To make salad, scatter spinach over the base of individual serving plates. Combine meat, beans, sesame seeds, cooked meat juices and dressing in a bowl, toss lightly and divide equally among individual plates. Spoon over any remaining dressing.

Serve with chargrilled vegetables, rice or pasta.

Beef, Tomato and Basil Salad with Spicy Soy Dressing

SERVES 4–6

Meat is only one ingredient of a well-balanced, nutritious meal. Try to serve less meat when you cook, and use more vegetables.

dressing

2 tablespoons lime juice
1 small chilli, seeded and finely chopped
3 tablespoons low-salt soy sauce
2 tablespoons apple juice concentrate
1 tablespoon fish sauce
1 clove garlic, crushed
1 cm piece fresh ginger, peeled, crushed

500–750 g lean beef
1 green zucchini, ends removed, halved and cut into thin julienne
1 yellow zucchini, ends removed, halved and cut into thin julienne
1 red capsicum, seeded and cut into long, thin strips
150 g red cherry tomatoes, halved
150 g yellow pear tomatoes, halved
1 cup basil leaves
¼ cup mint leaves
¼ cup coriander leaves

- To make dressing, place all ingredients in a jar and shake well.
- Chargrill beef on both sides until brown but still a little pink on the inside. (Depending on the thickness, the meat only needs a couple of minutes on each side if you like it rare.) Leave the beef to rest before slicing thinly and save any cooked meat juices to add to the dressing.
- Blanch zucchini and capsicum.

- To make salad, combine all ingredients and add dressing. Toss lightly, being careful not to squash the tomatoes, and serve. Alternatively, you can serve the salad on individual plates. Divide beef evenly among plates and arrange decoratively in a circular pattern. Pile the salad and dressing in the centre of the beef and spoon over any remaining juices.

Serve with chargrilled vegetables, rice or pasta.

Beef, Tomato and Feta Salad with Basil Balsamic Dressing

SERVES 4–6

Fresh fragrant basil and the woodiness of balsamic vinegar are perfect taste complements to the beef and tomatoes.

dressing
2 tablespoons Balsamic Vinaigrette (page 128)
2 tablespoons finely chopped basil leaves

600–800 g lean beef
8 Roma tomatoes, cut into wedges
2 red onions, peeled and diced
200 g salad greens, washed and dried
150 g low-fat feta cheese, crumbled
freshly ground black pepper
extra basil leaves

- To make dressing, place all ingredients in a jar and shake well. Add the basil.
- Chargrill beef on both sides until brown but still a little pink on the inside. (Depending on the thickness, the meat only needs a couple of minutes on each side if you like it rare.) Leave the beef to rest before slicing thinly and save any cooked meat juices to add to the dressing.
- To make salad, combine beef, tomatoes and onions. Add the dressing and toss lightly.
- Arrange salad greens on a salad platter and top with the beef mixture. Add the crumbled feta and black pepper, and garnish with extra basil leaves.

This salad is best served on its own.

Beetroot and Spinach Salad with Raspberry Vinegar

SERVES 4–6

For us, holidays at the beach inevitably mean a trip to the Queenscliff and Point Lonsdale Sunday markets. It was at one of these markets that I first tasted raspberry vinegar, which I then discovered went with all sorts of dishes. It is easy to make, and you can add it to a basic green salad or a Stone Fruit Salad for a really delicious flavour. In this recipe, the vinegar really brings out the flavours of the cooked beetroot.

$1/2$ cup Raspberry Vinegar (page 140)
1.5 kg beetroot
1 large bunch spinach
2 tablespoons chopped walnuts
250 g fresh raspberries

- Make the dressing as instructed and set aside.
- Cut tops from beetroots and wash thoroughly. Place in a saucepan, cover with water and cook for about 45 minutes. Allow to cool slightly before removing skin and cutting each beetroot into quarters. Place warm beetroot in a bowl and add raspberry vinegar. Cover and allow to cool and stand for at least an hour.
- Prepare spinach as for salad greens.
- To make salad, place spinach in a bowl or on a platter. Add beetroot, walnuts and raspberries, and spoon over any remaining beetroot and raspberry vinegar juices. Serve.

Serve with chicken, lamb or chargrilled vegetables.

Beetroot with Honey, Soy and Sesame Dressing

SERVES 4-6

Simple and so, so delicious!

$1/4$ cup Honey, Soy and Sesame Dressing (page 135)
1 kg beetroot

- Make the dressing as instructed and set aside.
- Cut tops from beetroots and wash thoroughly. Place in a saucepan, cover with water and cook for about 45 minutes. Allow to cool slightly before removing skin and cutting each beetroot into quarters. Place warm beetroot in a bowl and add dressing. Cover and allow to cool and stand for at least an hour.

Serve with chicken, lamb, chargrilled vegetables or Salad of Greens (page 97).

Borlotti Bean and Tuna Salad

SERVES 4-6

I never leave for holidays without at least a couple of cans of borlotti beans. Add leftover vegetables, chopped fresh vegetables or a can of tuna and you have a quick and healthy salad. You can also use cold leftover fish.

2 tablespoons Vinaigrette (page 146)
1 bunch watercress
4 cups cooked borlotti beans*
1 × 425 g can tuna in springwater, drained
1 red capsicum, seeded and chopped
2 sticks celery, finely chopped
1 salad onion, peeled and finely chopped
1 cup roughly chopped parsley
juice of $1/2$ lemon
freshly ground pepper

* If using canned beans, drain well and rinse off excess salt by running the beans under cold water in a sieve and drain again. If using dried beans, check the pack for cooking instructions. Beans will generally need to be soaked overnight, covered with fresh water and cooked gently for a couple of hours until tender.

- Make the dressing as instructed and set aside.
- Prepare watercress as for salad greens and use to line a serving platter.
- To make salad, combine beans, tuna, capsicum, celery, onion and parsley in a large bowl and add dressing. Toss lightly, pour over lemon juice, add pepper to taste, and place on the watercress.

This salad is best served as a main meal.

Brown Rice and Vegetable Salad

SERVES 4–6

Brown rice has three times more fibre than white rice, but it's the nutty texture that makes it perfect for this salad.

dressing
2 teaspoons white wine vinegar
a pinch of salt or cayenne pepper
freshly ground black pepper
2 tablespoons safflower oil

3 cups cold cooked brown rice
1 medium carrot, finely chopped
1 cup cold cooked peas
1 small red chilli, seeded and finely chopped
1 small red capsicum, seeded and finely chopped
1 small yellow capsicum, seeded and finely chopped
2 spring onions, finely chopped
1 tablespoon finely chopped basil
1 tablespoon finely grated parmesan cheese (optional)

- To make dressing, place all ingredients except the oil in a jar and shake well. Pour into a small bowl and slowly whisk in the oil.
- To make salad, combine all ingredients and add dressing. Toss lightly and serve.

Serve with chicken, fish, turkey, chargrilled vegetables, Salad of Greens (page 97) or radicchio.

Brown Rice, Spinach and Feta Salad with Honey, Soy and Sesame Dressing

SERVES 4–6

This salad is perfect for the sportsperson in the family, as it is power-packed with iron, protein, vitamins, minerals and high-energy carbohydrates. You can use cubes of tofu or balls of low-fat ricotta cheese (see this page) in place of the feta.

2 tablespoons Honey, Soy and Sesame Dressing (page 135)
300 g baby spinach leaves
2 cups cold cooked brown rice
1 small red chilli, seeded and finely chopped (optional)
200 g low-fat feta cheese, cubed
2 tablespoons finely chopped chives

- Make the dressing as instructed and set aside.
- Prepare spinach as for salad greens. Blanch and chop roughly.
- To make salad, combine all ingredients and add dressing. Toss lightly, being careful not to break up the feta, and serve.
- To make ricotta balls, drain ricotta well, take a small spoonful and roll in the palm of your hand to make small firm balls. These balls can be rolled in finely chopped parsley or chives, or poppy and sesame seeds.

Serve the salad with chargrilled vegetables, fish or Pawpaw, Mango and Pineapple Salad (page 83).

Caesar Salad

SERVES 4-6

When my family holidays at the beach we must have at least one Caesar Salad at Angelina's Café in Point Lonsdale (I dare not ask about the fat content!). Caesar salads are notoriously high in fat, but a favourite salad of so many people. My adaptation is close to the original in taste, but with nowhere near as much fat.

dressing

1 cup low-fat yoghurt
1 tablespoon low-fat, cholesterol-free commercial mayonnaise (page 5)
1 tablespoon apple juice concentrate
2 teaspoons–1 tablespoon fish sauce
$1/4$ teaspoon dry mustard
$1/4$ teaspoon pepper

400 g cos (romaine) lettuce leaves (choose inner, young green leaves)
$1/2$ loaf day-old wholemeal or white high-fibre bread
1 tablespoon olive oil
1 tablespoon fish sauce
2 cloves garlic, crushed
6–8 hard-boiled eggs (whites only), roughly chopped
$1/3$ cup grated parmesan cheese
$1/4$ cup finely chopped chives

- To make dressing, place all ingredients in a glass jar and shake well. Taste the dressing using just 2 teaspoons fish sauce and add more if you are looking for a saltier taste. There is fish sauce in the croutons, and after a few mouthfuls of salad you can certainly taste the fish sauce, so use sparingly.
- Prepare lettuce as for salad greens. Dry the leaves thoroughly.
- Preheat the oven to 180°C.

Julie Stafford's Salads

- Cut bread into slices, remove crusts, cut into cubes and place in a bowl. Combine oil, fish sauce and garlic, pour over the bread and toss well. Spread the bread onto a non-stick baking tray and bake until golden brown. Or toast on both sides under a griller.
- To make salad, combine all ingredients in a large bowl, toss and serve immediately.

This salad is best served on its own.

Carrot and Currant Salad with Orange Curry Vinaigrette

SERVES 4–6

This salad tastes great on top of a baked potato with cottage cheese.

dressing
1/2 cup freshly squeezed orange juice
2 tablespoons white wine vinegar
1 1/2 teaspoons curry powder or 1 teaspoon vindaloo curry paste
  (page 11)
1/4 teaspoon ground cumin
1/4 teaspoon finely chopped fresh ginger
1/4 teaspoon finely chopped red chilli
1 teaspoon honey
1 small shallot, peeled and finely chopped or 1 tablespoon finely
  chopped chives or parsley

1 kg carrots
1 cup currants
1/4 cup finely chopped parsley

- To make dressing, place all ingredients in a jar and shake well.
- Wash carrots and lightly scrub to remove any dirt. The carrots can be grated, cut into thin julienne or sliced into thin rounds. Blanch carrots.
- To make salad, combine all ingredients in a large bowl, toss lightly, and allow to stand for at least an hour before serving.

Serve with chicken, fish, beef, lamb, chargrilled vegetables, or Potato Salad with Mustard Mayo Dressing (page 87).

Opposite: Beef, Tomato and Feta Salad with Basil Balsamic Dressing (see page 32)

Carrot and Thyme Salad with Citrus Vinaigrette

SERVES 4–6

I like to leave just a little of the green tops on the baby carrots for presentation.

2 tablespoons Citrus Vinaigrette (page 129)
1.5 kg baby carrots
$^1/_4$–$^1/_2$ cup thyme leaves

- Make the dressing as instructed and set aside.
- Wash carrots and lightly scrub to remove any dirt. Blanch carrots.
- To make salad, combine all ingredients in a large bowl, toss lightly, and allow to stand for at least an hour before serving.

Serve with chicken, fish, beef, lamb, chargrilled vegetables, baked potato or Potato Salad with Mustard Mayo Dressing (page 87).

Opposite: Caesar Salad (see page 38)

Chargrilled Carrot, Zucchini and Parsnip Salad

SERVES 4–6

If you love parsnips, then this salad is for you. Serve with salad greens and make a meal of it.

2 tablespoons Vinaigrette (page 146)
4 carrots, tops removed
4 zucchinis, ends removed
4 parsnips, tops removed and peeled
1 tablespoon finely chopped fresh ginger
1 tablespoon crushed garlic
1/4 cup chopped coriander leaves
freshly ground black pepper

- Make the dressing as instructed and set aside.
- Cut vegetables into four lengthwise and toss with ginger and garlic for at least 2 hours prior to chargrilling.
- To make salad, combine vegetables, coriander, pepper to taste and dressing. Toss lightly and serve.

Serve with chicken, fish, beef, lamb, Couscous Salad (page 53) or Salad of Greens (page 97).

Chicken and Snow Pea Salad with Mango Curry Dressing

SERVES 4–6

A salad that is easy to make and full of lovely warm and fruity flavours. Try to make this salad at least once in summer, when mangoes are at their best.

dressing
1 teaspoon finely chopped fresh ginger
1 large mango, peeled and chopped
1 cup low-fat yoghurt
1 tablespoon low-fat, cholesterol-free commercial mayonnaise (page 5)
1 teaspoon cumin
$1/2$–1 teaspoon curry powder or 1 teaspoon vindaloo curry paste
   (page 11)

500–750 g chicken fillets, skin and fat removed
500 g snow peas, topped and tailed
coriander or basil leaves

- To make dressing, place all ingredients in a blender and process until smooth.
- Chargrill or steam the chicken until cooked. Thinly slice and set aside until cool.
- While chicken is cooking, blanch the snowpeas.
- To make salad, arrange snow peas on a platter and top with the chicken. Add dressing and garnish with coriander or basil leaves.

Serve with Salad of Greens (page 97), Roasted Sweet Potato and Rosemary Salad (page 95), chargrilled vegetables or radicchio.

Chicken, Carrot and Cashew with Honey, Soy and Sesame Dressing

SERVES 4–6

I like lots of coriander in this salad. If this is the first time you use this herb, start with a small amount – it has quite a unique, assertive flavour. If you haven't acquired a taste for it, substitute chives or basil. The salad makes an ideal lunch, or serve as a meal on a hot, balmy summer's evening.

2 tablespoons Honey, Soy and Sesame Dressing (page 135)
600–750 g chicken fillets, skin and fat removed
200–300 g curly endive
1 red onion, peeled and sliced thinly
200 g carrots, cut into very thin rounds, blanched
$^{1}/_{2}$ cup raw cashews
1–2 tablespoons chopped coriander
1 tablespoon chopped mint
coriander leaves (extra)

- Make the dressing as instructed and set aside.
- Chargrill the chicken. Cover and keep warm. When you are ready to assemble the salad, slice each fillet into 8 pieces and spoon over any remaining cooking juices.
- Prepare endive as for salad greens.
- To make salad, mix together all the ingredients except the endive and extra coriander while the chicken is still warm and toss lightly. Place the endive on a platter or individual plates and top with the chicken mixture. Garnish with the remaining coriander leaves and serve.

Serve with fresh orange, grapefruit, pineapple or mango slices.

Chicken, Spinach and Hazelnut Salad with Feta

SERVES 4–6

The fresh, crunchy and creamy flavours of spinach, hazelnuts and feta help to enhance the simple flavours of a chicken cooked in its own juices.

dressing
2 teaspoons balsamic vinegar
1–2 cloves garlic, crushed
a pinch of salt
2 tablespoons olive oil
1 tablespoon finely chopped hazelnuts

800 g–1 kg chicken fillets, skin and fat removed
200 g baby spinach leaves
6 spring onions, diagonally sliced
50 g low-fat feta cheese, crumbled
freshly ground black pepper

- To make dressing, place all ingredients except the oil in a jar and shake well. Pour into a small bowl and slowly whisk in the oil. Add hazelnuts.
- Chargrill or steam the chicken until cooked. Slice thinly and set aside (ensure it stays warm).
- To make salad, combine spinach, chicken, spring onions and some of the dressing in a salad bowl and toss lightly. Spoon onto a salad platter. Scatter over the feta, remaining dressing, pepper to taste and serve immediately.

Serve with chargrilled vegetables, Salad of Greens (page 97) or radicchio.

Chicken, Sultana and Pinenut Salad with Mustard Vinaigrette

SERVES 4–6

The combination of fruits, nuts and the sharp flavour of mustard really livens up this chicken salad.

2 tablespoons Mustard Vinaigrette (page 138)
800 g–1 kg chicken fillets, skin and fat removed
200 g mixed salad greens
$1/2$ cup pinenuts
6 spring onions, diagonally sliced
2 Granny Smith apples, cored and diced or 2 pears, cored and diced
1 cup sultanas
freshly ground black pepper

- Make the dressing as instructed and set aside.
- Chargrill or steam the chicken until cooked. Slice thinly and set aside (ensure it stays warm).
- Wash and dry salad greens thoroughly.
- Dry-roast pinenuts if desired.
- To make salad, combine lettuce, chicken, spring onions, apples or pears, sultanas, pinenuts, pepper to taste and dressing in a salad bowl and toss lightly. Spoon onto a platter and serve.

Serve with chargrilled vegetables.

Chickpea and Macaroni Salad with Italian Vinaigrette

SERVES 4-6

You can use canned chickpeas for this recipe, to save time. If using dried chickpeas, soak them overnight in cold water. The next day, drain and discard the water, add fresh water and simmer until tender.

dressing

2 teaspoons balsamic vinegar
1–2 cloves garlic, crushed
1 Roma tomato, peeled, seeded and finely chopped
a pinch of salt
a pinch of pepper
2 tablespoons olive oil

2 cups chickpeas
2–3 cups cooked macaroni
1 red capsicum, chargrilled (page 13) and roughly chopped
1 yellow capsicum, chargrilled and roughly chopped
1 green capsicum, chargrilled and roughly chopped
1 salad onion, peeled and sliced into thin wedges
200 g cherry tomatoes, halved
1/2 cup basil leaves
2 tablespoons grated parmesan cheese
freshly ground black pepper

- To make dressing, place all ingredients except the oil in a jar and shake well. Pour into a small bowl and slowly whisk in the oil.
- To make salad, combine all ingredients and add dressing. Toss lightly and serve.

Serve with chargrilled vegetables, Salad of Greens (page 97) or radicchio.

Chickpea and Orange Salad with Tahini Dressing

SERVES 4–6

Chickpeas are a most valuable source of quality vegetable protein, and they make an ideal meat substitute. They have a wide range of vitamins and minerals, including a less common one, copper.

dressing
200 ml low-fat yoghurt
2 tablespoons tahini (page 10)
1 tablespoon honey
2 tablespoons lemon juice
1 teaspoon finely grated lemon rind

4 cups cooked chickpeas*
2 navel oranges, peeled and cubed
1 cup sultanas, raisins or chopped dates
2 sticks celery, finely chopped
1 red capsicum, seeded and chopped
1 cup dry-roasted pecans, chopped
1 cup finely chopped spring onions

* If using canned chickpeas, drain well, rinse off excess salt by running under cold water in a sieve and drain again. If using dried chickpeas, check the pack for cooking instructions. Dried chickpeas will generally need to be soaked overnight, covered with fresh water, and cooked gently for a couple of hours until tender.

- To make dressing, place all ingredients in a glass jar and shake well.
- To make salad, combine all ingredients in a large bowl and add dressing. Toss lightly and serve.

variations

For Chicken, Chickpea and Orange Salad with Tahini Dressing, add 300–500 g chopped chicken (remove the fat and skin first).

For Lamb, Chickpea and Orange Salad with Tahini Dressing, add 300–500 g cooked, slightly rare, chargrilled lamb that has been thinly sliced; ¼ cup finely chopped coriander leaves; and for garnish, 2 tablespoons mint leaves.

Serve with Salad of Greens (page 97).

Chinese Corn and Vegetable Salad with Shiitake Mushrooms

SERVES 4-6

Field mushrooms can be used in place of the shiitake.

dressing
1 teaspoon finely chopped ginger
2 tablespoons finely chopped chives
2 teaspoons fish sauce
1 teaspoon five-spice powder (page 4)
1 tablespoon apple juice concentrate
$1/4$ cup Chinese wine or dry sherry
$1/2$ cup freshly squeezed orange juice

150 g dried shiitake mushrooms, thinly sliced
200 g baby bok choy
250 g green beans, sliced diagonally
125 g snow peas, topped and tailed
200 g baby sweet corn
1 yellow capsicum, seeded and cut into long strips
3 sticks celery, diagonally sliced
2 red onions, peeled and thinly sliced
200 g bean sprouts
2 tablespoons finely chopped chives

- To make dressing, place all ingredients in a jar and shake well.
- Soak shiitake mushrooms in lukewarm water for about 20 minutes to soften. Drain well, remove the woody stems and slice thinly.
- Blanch bok choy, beans, snow peas, sweet corn and capsicum separately.

Julie Stafford's Salads

- To make salad, combine all ingredients except chives. Add dressing and allow to stand for about an hour. Garnish with chives and serve.

Serve with beef, lamb, chicken, fish, prawns, scallops or chargrilled vegetables.

Coleslaw with Orange Vindaloo Dressing

SERVES 4–6

Coleslaw need no longer be a grated mixture of vegetables sitting in a bath of oily mayonnaise. This recipe is an example of what a coleslaw can become with good ingredients and a little imagination.

dressing
1 cup freshly squeezed orange juice
1 teaspoon vindaloo curry paste (page 11)
1 small red chilli, seeded, finely chopped
1 tablespoon low-fat, cholesterol-free commercial mayonnaise (page 5)
$1/2$ cup finely chopped chives

500 g cabbage, finely shredded
2 navel oranges, peeled and segmented
$1/2$ cup dried apricots, roughly chopped
$1/2$ cup dried peaches, roughly chopped
$1/2$ cup sultanas
$1/2$ cup chopped mixed dry-roasted nuts (e.g. cashews, peanuts, brazils)
1 tablespoon sesame seeds
2 spring onions, finely sliced
2 sticks celery, finely sliced

- To make dressing, place all ingredients in a glass jar and shake well.
- To make salad, combine all ingredients and add dressing. Toss lightly, stand for at least an hour and serve.

Serve with chargrilled vegetables, roasted rosemary potatoes, baked potato, beef, lamb or chicken.

Couscous Salad

SERVES 4-6

This is a Middle Eastern-style salad that uses a popular staple, couscous, and the fragrant spice, cumin. You can cook the couscous the day before if you like and keep it refrigerated.

dressing
3/4 cup freshly squeezed orange juice
1/4 cup freshly squeezed lemon juice
1-2 teaspoons cumin
1 tablespoon olive oil

500 g couscous
2 cups boiling water
2 cups finely chopped spring onions
1 small cucumber, peeled and seeded
1/2 red capsicum, seeded and chopped
1/2 yellow capsicum, seeded and chopped
1 cup dry-roasted pinenuts or peanuts
1 cup sultanas
1/2 cup finely chopped fresh mint

- To make dressing, place all ingredients except the oil in a screw-top jar and shake well. Pour into a small bowl and slowly whisk in the oil.
- Place couscous in a metal or ceramic bowl. Pour over boiling water, stir a little, cover and stand until all the water has been absorbed. Use a fork to fluff up the couscous before adding the other ingredients and dressing.
- To make salad, combine all ingredients in a large bowl. Add the dressing, toss lightly and serve.

Serve with fish, chicken, lamb or chargrilled vegetables.

Egg and Lettuce Salad with Creamy Mayo Dressing

SERVES 4–6

This classic salad is a favourite in our household. To cut back on saturated fats, discard all the egg yolks, or at least half of them.

1 cup Creamy Mayonnaise (page 130)
1 iceberg lettuce
10 hard-boiled eggs
2 yellow capsicums, seeded
1 small red capsicum, seeded and cut into very thin slivers

- Make the dressing as instructed and set aside.
- Prepare lettuce as for salad greens and finely shred.
- Shell the eggs, cut in half and discard the yolks. Roughly chop the egg whites.
- Blanch or chargrill the yellow capsicums and chop roughly.
- To make salad, arrange lettuce on platter, spoon over half the dressing, add egg whites, yellow capsicum and the remaining dressing. Garnish with red capsicum and serve.

Serve with chicken, fish, beef, lamb, chargrilled vegetables or baked sweet potatoes.

Endive with Lemon and Herbs

SERVES 4–6

Endive is a frilly, frizzy-headed lettuce with a unique bitter flavour that is palate-cleansing.

dressing
lemon juice
freshly ground black pepper

600 g curly endive
$^1/_2$ cup finely chopped mixed herbs (e.g. parsley, basil, chives, dill, thyme, tarragon, oregano)

- Prepare endive as for salad greens. Blanch endive for a few seconds. Plunge into very cold water immediately.
- To make salad, combine all ingredients, add lemon juice and pepper to taste, toss lightly and serve.

Serve with chargrilled vegetables, fish, chicken, tomatoes or Avocado, Tomato and Carrot Salad (page 25).

Feta, Greens and Peanuts with Sweet Chilli Dressing

SERVES 4–6

You won't need a lot of feta to impart its lovely salty, sharp flavour to the salad. This soft uncooked cheese is pickled in brine and often included in Greek-style salads. Rinse under cold water before using to remove most of the salt.

1/4 cup Sweet Chilli Dressing (page 142)
100 g spinach leaves
100 g watercress
100 g baby bok choy leaves
300 g sugar peas, topped and tailed
100 g beans, topped, tailed and halved
100 g dry-roasted peanuts
150 g low-fat feta cheese, cubed or crumbled into large pieces
1 tablespoon chopped dill

- Make the dressing as instructed and set aside.
- Prepare spinach, watercress and bok choy as for salad greens.
- Blanch sugar peas and beans.
- To make salad, combine all ingredients except dill and add dressing. Toss lightly, garnish with dill and serve.

Serve with chargrilled vegetables or Roasted Roma Tomato and Thyme Salad (page 94).

Fish and Mango Salad with Thai Dressing

SERVES 4–6

The sweet flavour of mango goes magnificently with fish. The alliance is enhanced in this recipe with the addition of a spicy Asian-style dressing. Sea perch works well.

1/2 cup Thai Dressing (page 144)
1 cup fish stock or white wine
2 bay leaves
1 onion, peeled and diced
500–700 g firm fish fillets or marinara mix (calamari, prawns, octopus, mussels, fish pieces, crab)
1 red capsicum, seeded and chopped
1 yellow capsicum, seeded and chopped
1–2 mangoes, peeled and thinly sliced
200 g salad greens, washed and dried
1/4–1/2 cup chopped coriander

- Make the dressing as instructed and set aside.
- Place stock, bay leaves and onion into a small, shallow pan and bring to the boil. When boiling, add fish or marinara mix, stir, cover and cook until tender.
- To make salad, combine all ingredients and add dressing. Toss lightly and serve.

Serve with chargrilled vegetables or Salad of Greens (page 97).

Fish and Noodle Salad with Spicy Oriental Dressing

SERVES 4–6

The flavours in this salad intensify the longer it stands.

1 cup Spicy Oriental Dressing (page 142)
500–700 g firm fish fillets
1 red onion, peeled and diced
500 g thin spaghetti
1 red capsicum, seeded and cut into thin strips
1 carrot, cut into thin julienne
1 zucchini, cut into thin julienne
2 tablespoons cornflour
$1/4$ cup water
2 tablespoons of both coriander and mint, chopped

- Make the dressing as instructed, and use to marinate fish and onion at least 2 hours prior to cooking.
- Preheat the oven to 180°C.
- To cook fish, transfer fish, onion and marinade to a small, shallow, baking dish, cover and bake for about 20 minutes or until the fish is cooked through. Allow the fish to cool in the marinade. When cool, drain off the marinade and reserve. Break up the fish into bite-sized pieces and keep warm.
- While fish is cooking, break spaghetti in half and cook in boiling water until *al dente*. Drain and keep warm.
- Blanch capsicum, carrot and zucchini.
- Mix cornflour and water together and stir into the marinade. Bring to the boil, simmer and stir until it thickens. Allow to cool.
- To make salad, combine all ingredients and add dressing. Toss lightly and stand for at least an hour before serving.

Serve with chargrilled vegetables or Salad of Greens (page 97).

Fish Hawaii with Salad Greens

SERVES 4–6

I particularly like trevally in this recipe, but any other firm-fleshed fish is suitable.

dressing
$1/2$ cup unsweetened pineapple juice
1 tablespoon freshly squeezed lemon juice
1 tablespoon apple juice concentrate
1 tablespoon chopped pickled ginger (page 4)
1 teaspoon finely grated lemon rind
1 tablespoon finely chopped mint

500–700 g firm fish fillets
1 red capsicum, seeded and chopped
1 green capsicum, seeded and chopped
1 yellow capsicum, seeded and chopped
$1/4$–$1/2$ fresh pineapple, peeled, cored and chopped
200 g salad greens, washed and dried
extra mint leaves
extra coriander leaves

- To make dressing, combine all ingredients in a glass jar and shake well.
- Steam fish until cooked. Cool and break up the flesh into large pieces.
- Blanch capsicums.
- To make salad, combine fish, capsicums, pineapple, dressing and toss lightly. Arrange salad greens on a platter and add fish mixture. Garnish with extra mint or coriander.

This salad is best served on its own.

Ginger Lamb, Orange and Carrot Salad with Orange Chilli Dressing

SERVES 4–6

Choose spring lamb for this recipe, which will need only a minimum of cooking. The fillets should be a deep-pink colour.

dressing
$1/2$ cup Orange Chilli Dressing (page 139)
1 small red chilli, seeded and finely chopped

500–750 g lean lamb (e.g. lamb fillets, chump chops with bone and fat removed or loin roast)
1 tablespoon finely chopped fresh ginger
4 cloves garlic, peeled and crushed
2 carrots, halved and cut into thin julienne
100 g fresh or frozen peas
4 navel oranges, peeled and segmented
1 cup basil leaves
$1/2$ cup coriander leaves
$1/4$ cup mint leaves
4 spring onions, diagonally sliced

- Make the dressing as instructed, adding chilli. Set aside.
- Toss lamb in combined ginger and garlic and set aside for a few hours or cover and refrigerate overnight. Drain juices from the lamb and chargrill. Any remaining juices can be brought to the boil (add a little water or stock if necessary) and added to dressing.
- While lamb is cooking, blanch carrots and peas separately.
- Combine orange segments, carrots, peas, basil, coriander and mint.

- When lamb is cooked (slightly rare in the middle and brown on both sides), cut into thin slices. Add any remaining cooked meat juices to dressing.
- To make salad, combine all ingredients except the spring onions and add the dressing. Toss lightly, garnish with spring onions, and serve. Alternatively, portion the lamb onto individual plates, top with equal amounts of salad, spoon over dressing and garnish with spring onions.

Serve with chargrilled vegetables, rice or pasta.

Grapefruit, Mango, Avocado and Greens with Ginger Vinaigrette

SERVES 4-6

A tangy fruity combination with the sharp but warm taste of ginger. It is delicious served as an entrée or as a side dish to accompany cooked white meats or fish.

2 tablespoons Ginger Vinaigrette (page 134)
200 g mixed salad greens
2 pink or regular grapefruit, peeled and segmented
2 mangoes, peeled and thinly sliced
2 avocados, peeled and thinly sliced
1 tablespoon pickled ginger (page 4)
$1/4$ cup coriander leaves

- Make the dressing as instructed and set aside.
- Wash and dry salad greens thoroughly.
- To make salad, combine all ingredients in a large bowl. Add dressing and serve.

Serve with chicken, fish, prawns or calamari.

Greek Salad

SERVES 4–6

An oldie, but a goodie.

2 tablespoons Vinaigrette (page 146)
1 iceberg lettuce
1 burpless cucumber, halved lengthwise, seeded and diagonally sliced
2 sticks celery, diagonally sliced
1 green capsicum, seeded, halved and diagonally sliced
3 tomatoes, quartered
1 salad onion, peeled and sliced into thin rounds
8–12 black olives, pitted and halved
80–100 g low-fat feta cheese, crumbled or cubed

- Make the dressing as instructed and set aside.
- Remove outer leaves from lettuce and discard. Cut lettuce in half, remove core and chop up roughly. Wash and dry thoroughly.
- To make salad, place lettuce at the bottom of a bowl, add the other ingredients and dressing. Toss lightly and serve.

Serve with fish or pasta.

Green Coriander Fruit Salad with Citrus Vinaigrette

SERVES 4–6

The chives, mint and coriander give a refreshing lift to this green-on-green fruit salad.

2 tablespoons Citrus Vinaigrette (page 143)
2 Granny Smith apples, cored and sliced into thin segments
2 cups large green grapes, halved
4 kiwifruit, peeled and sliced into thin rounds
1/4 honeydew melon, peeled, seeded and thinly sliced
1 grapefruit, peeled and segmented
1/4 cup mint leaves
2 tablespoons finely chopped coriander
1 tablespoon finely chopped chives

- Make the dressing as instructed and set aside.
- To make salad, arrange ingredients decoratively in a bowl. Add dressing and allow to stand for at least an hour before serving.

Serve with chicken, fish, prawns, calamari or Pawpaw, Mango and Pineapple Salad (page 83).

Green Fruit Salad

SERVES 4–6

sweet syrup
zest of 2 lemons
1 cup Sweet Syrup (page 146)

200 g peeled, seeded and sliced honeydew melon
100 g peeled, cored and thinly sliced pineapple
200 g kiwifruit, peeled and sliced
100 g green grapes, stems removed
200 g Granny Smith apples, cored and sliced
100 g pears, cored and sliced

- Wash lemons and, using a citrus zester, remove long strips of zest. If you don't have a zester you can remove the peel with a sharp knife or vegetable peeler, being careful not to remove too much of the pith. Cut the peel into long thin strips.
- Make the sweet syrup as instructed and add the zest while syrup is still warm.
- To make salad, combine fruits in a bowl, and pour over the cooled sweet syrup.

Serve with low-fat ice-cream, low-fat yoghurt or low-fat fruit sorbet.

Hot Tropical Fruit Salad

SERVES 4–6

Island fruits conjure up visions of sunny days, rolling seas and relaxed living. Most of us, however, can enjoy these fruit combinations all year around without so much as leaving our front door.

sweet syrup
1 cup Sweet Ginger Syrup (page 148)
1 tablespoon finely chopped glacé ginger

100 g peeled, seeded and sliced honeydew melon
100 g green grapes, stems removed
100 g black grapes, stems removed
100 g peeled and sliced mango
100 g peeled, seeded and sliced pawpaw
200 g peeled, cored and thinly sliced pineapple
$^1/_2$ cup grated fresh coconut or shredded coconut, and/or lime zest

- Make sweet ginger syrup as instructed, adding glacé ginger while the syrup is still warm.
- To make salad, combine fruits in a bowl, pour over cooled syrup and garnish with coconut and/or lime zest.

Serve with low-fat ice-cream, low-fat yoghurt or low-fat fruit sorbet.

Iceberg and Radicchio Wedges with Vinaigrette

SERVES 4–6

Sometimes a great salad is nothing more than a mix of one or two ingredients presented in a less usual way. You can't go wrong if the ingredients are 'just-picked' fresh.

2 tablespoons Vinaigrette (page 146)
1 head iceberg lettuce
1 head radicchio
1 cup chopped chives

- Make the dressing as instructed and set aside.
- Remove outer leaves from the lettuces and discard. Cut lettuces into 8 wedges and remove central core. Wash thoroughly and drain the leaves cut-side down on paper towels or a tea towel.
- To make salad, arrange the different coloured lettuce wedges decoratively on a platter and scatter over the chives. Pour over the dressing and serve.

Serve with chargrilled vegetables, beef, lamb, chicken, turkey, fish, Potato Salad with Mustard Mayo Dressing (page 87), rice or pasta.

Lamb and Pesto Salad

SERVES 4-6

You need only a little pesto to capture the flavour and essence of Italy in this delicious recipe.

dressing
2 tablespoons Vinaigrette (page 146)
1 teaspoon pesto (page 8)

500–750 g lean lamb (e.g. lamb fillets, leg of lamb, chump chops with bone and fat removed)
1 tablespoon crushed garlic
1 teaspoon pesto (page 8)
200 g baby spinach leaves, chopped
4 sticks celery, washed and diagonally sliced
2 red apples, cored and thinly sliced
$1/2$ cup currants
$1/4$ cup pinenuts
$1/4$ cup basil leaves, torn
1–2 tablespoons grated fresh parmesan cheese

- Make the dressing as instructed, adding the pesto. Set aside.
- Marinate lamb in garlic and pesto for at least 2 hours.
- Chargrill lamb. When cooked, the lamb should be still slightly rare in the middle and brown on both sides. Rest before slicing thinly. Add any remaining cooked meat juices to dressing.
- Blanch spinach.
- To make salad, combine all ingredients except the parmesan. Add dressing, toss lightly, turn out onto a serving platter and garnish with parmesan.

Serve with chargrilled vegetables.

Lamb Salad with Orange, Mango and Walnut Dressing

SERVES 4–6

There are so many wonderful flavours happening in this salad that it is best served as a main meal so that you can savour each without further distraction.

dressing
2 tablespoons Vinaigrette (page 146)
1 teaspoon finely grated orange zest
1–2 tablespoons chopped walnuts

500–750 g lean lamb (e.g. lamb fillets, leg of lamb, chump chops with bone and fat removed)
1–2 tablespoons grainy mustard
3 oranges, peeled and sliced into rounds
200 g mixed lettuce leaves, thoroughly washed
1–2 zucchinis, ends removed and sliced into thin rounds
2 mangoes, peeled and thinly sliced
$1/2$ cup mint leaves

- Make the dressing as instructed, adding orange zest and walnuts. Set aside.
- Combine lamb and mustard and allow to stand for at least 2 hours. Chargrill lamb. When cooked, the lamb should be still slightly rare in the middle and brown on both sides. Rest before cutting into thin slices. Add any remaining cooked meat juices to the dressing.
- To make salad, arrange orange slices decoratively around the edge of a salad platter. Combine all other ingredients, add dressing, toss lightly and turn out onto the centre of the oranges.

This salad is best served on its own.

Lamb, Spinach and Mint Salad with Spicy Soy Dressing

SERVES 4-6

Spring lamb, which is sweet, juicy and very tender, is ideal for this dish.

dressing

2 tablespoons lime juice
1 small chilli, seeded and finely chopped
3 tablespoons low-salt soy sauce
2 tablespoons apple juice concentrate
1 tablespoon fish sauce
1 clove garlic, crushed
1 teaspoon finely chopped fresh ginger

200 g baby spinach leaves
100 g snow peas, topped and tailed
100 g carrot, cut into thin rounds
1 red capsicum, seeded and cut into long thin strips
500–750 g lean lamb (e.g. lamb fillets, leg of lamb, chump chops with
    bone and fat removed)
1 red onion, peeled and thinly sliced
1/2 cup mint leaves
1 tablespoon chopped dill

- To make dressing, place all ingredients in a glass jar and shake well.
- Prepare spinach as for salad greens.
- Blanch snow peas, carrot and capsicum separately.
- Chargrill lamb. When cooked, the lamb should be still slightly rare in the middle and brown on both sides. Rest before cutting into thin slices. Add any remaining cooked meat juices to the dressing.

- To make salad, combine all ingredients and add dressing. Toss lightly and serve. Alternatively, you can serve the salad on individual plates. Divide dressed salad evenly among plates and arrange lamb decoratively on top. Spoon over any remaining juices.

Serve with chargrilled vegetables, roasted rosemary potatoes, rice or pasta.

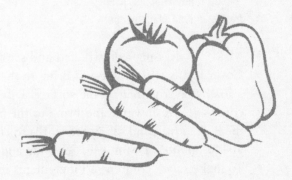

Lentil Summer Salad

Lentils are an excellent source of protein and make an ideal vegetarian meal. Unlike other pulses, lentils make a fast meal, as they don't generally need to be soaked before cooking. As a rule, 2 cups of raw lentils yield approximately 4 cups cooked. This salad is full of fibre, vitamins and minerals.

2 tablespoons Garlic Vinaigrette (page 133)
2 cups brown lentils
1 cup finely chopped spring onions
4 Roma tomatoes, peeled, seeded and chopped
$1/2$ cucumber, peeled, seeded and chopped
1 red capsicum, seeded and chopped
1 yellow capsicum, seeded and chopped
2 small carrots, diced
$1/4$ cup finely chopped mint
$1/4$ cup finely chopped parsley
freshly ground black pepper

- Make the dressing as instructed and set aside.
- Cover lentils with water and bring to the boil. You'll notice a foamy layer gather on the surface. Discard this water, cover with fresh water and bring to the boil again. Lower the heat, cover, and allow the lentils to cook until tender, 20–40 minutes. Drain well. Set aside and keep warm.
- To make salad, combine all ingredients in a large bowl. Toss lightly and serve.

Serve with Salad of Greens (page 97) or chargrilled vegetables.

Opposite: Chicken, Carrot and Cashew with Honey, Soy and Sesame Dressing (see page 44)

Mandarin, Mango and Lychee Fruit Salad

SERVES 4–6

This salad works well as a dessert or, for a change, you may like to serve it with chargrilled chicken. The lychees add an interesting nutty texture and a sweet flavour.

sweet syrup
1 cup Sweet Orange Marmalade Syrup (page 148)
zest of 1 mandarin

1 × 565 g can lychees in light syrup
3 mandarins, peeled and segmented
400 g peeled and sliced mango flesh

- Wash mandarin and, using a citrus zester, remove strips of zest. If you don't have a zester you can remove peel with a sharp knife or vegetable peeler, being careful not to remove too much of the pith. Cut the peel into long thin strips.
- Drain lychees and reserve syrup.
- Make Sweet Orange Marmalade Syrup as instructed and add mandarin zest while the syrup is still warm.
- To make salad, combine fruits and pour over the cooled syrup.

Serve with low-fat ice-cream, low-fat yoghurt or low-fat fruit sorbet.

Opposite: Hot Tropical Fruit Salad (see page 66)

Marinara Rice Salad

SERVES 4-6

It wasn't until this favourite risotto was allowed to go cold one day that I realised what a wonderful rice salad it made. Served with plenty of salad greens or radicchio, it is a meal on its own or a good one to add variety at a barbecue.

1 tablespoon finely chopped fresh ginger
1 teaspoon sweet chilli sauce (page 10)
1 tablespoon sesame oil
2 brown onions, peeled and cut into wedges
200 g carrots, sliced into thin rounds
2 cups Arborio (short-grain Italian) rice
1 litre hot stock (vegetable, fish or chicken)
1/2 cup dry white wine
1 kg marinara mix (calamari, prawns, fish pieces, mussels, octopus)
1/4 cup finely chopped chives
1/4 cup finely chopped parsley
1/2 red capsicum, seeded and cut into thin strips
1-2 tablespoons chopped coriander

- Place ginger, chilli sauce, sesame oil, onions and carrots into a cold, large non-stick frying pan. Cover and cook over a gentle heat for 7–10 minutes or until the onions and carrots begin to soften.
- Add rice, hot stock and wine. Stir, cover and cook gently until the rice is nearly cooked. Lift the lid and stir a couple of times to make sure the rice is not sticking to the base of the pan.
- Add marinara mix and stir through the hot rice. Cover and continue cooking until the fish is cooked through, the rice *al dente* and all the cooking liquid absorbed. Once again, it is a good idea to lift the lid to stir the mixture a couple of times, being careful not to break up or overcook the fish.

- Remove the rice mixture from the pan, and transfer to a platter. Cover and allow to cool.
- Just before serving, garnish with chives, parsley, capsicum and coriander.

Serve with Salad of Greens (page 97), chargrilled vegetables, Roasted Roma Tomato and Thyme Salad (page 94) or radicchio.

Melon Glory Fruit Salad

SERVES 4–6

It doesn't take too much to turn this sweet salad into a spicy one – just add some pickled ginger (page 4) and some chopped coriander before serving and stir through.

sweet syrup
zest of 1 orange
1 cup Sweet Syrup (page 146)

300 g watermelon balls
300 g honeydew melon balls
300 g cantaloupe (muskmelon) balls

- Wash orange and, using a citrus zester, remove long strips of zest. If you don't have a zester you can remove peel with a sharp knife or vegetable peeler, being careful not to remove too much of the pith. Cut peel into long thin strips.
- Make the sweet syrup as instructed, adding the orange zest while the syrup is still warm.
- To make salad, combine fruits and pour over the cooled syrup.

Serve with low-fat ice-cream, low-fat yoghurt or low-fat fruit sorbet.

Mushroom and Parsley Salad

SERVES 4–6

Often referred to as the vegetarian's meat, the compact little mushroom is an extremely nutritious food, and is particularly rich in B-group vitamins and iron. I have used the cultivated mushroom for convenience, but a combination of fresh and dried varieties will work as well, especially for a dinner party.

2 tablespoons Vinaigrette (page 146)
500–700 g cultivated mushrooms, washed, dried and sliced thinly
1 cup finely chopped parsley
1 cup finely chopped spring onions

- Make the dressing as instructed and set aside.
- To make salad, combine mushrooms, parsley and dressing. Toss well and frequently and allow to marinate for at least 2 hours. Add spring onions before serving.

Serve with chargrilled vegetables, beef, lamb, chicken, turkey, fish, Potato Salad with Mustard Mayo Dressing (page 87), rice or pasta.

Orange, Apricot, Peach and Passionfruit Salad

SERVES 4-6

It is probably enough just to sit on a balmy summer's evening and enjoy the sweet oozing juices of a fresh summer peach, but then we'd miss out on the many wonderful taste sensations that occur when we marry them with other summer favourites.

sweet syrup
2 oranges (Valencias or Jaffas)
2 cups Sweet Syrup (page 146)

10 apricots, halved and stoned
4 peaches, stoned and quartered
pulp and juice of 12 passionfruit

- Wash oranges and, using a citrus zester, remove long strips of zest. If you don't have a zester you can remove the peel with a sharp knife or vegetable peeler, being careful not to remove too much of the pith. Cut peel into long thin strips.
- Make the sweet syrup as instructed and add zest to the hot syrup. Cook, stirring continuously, for a couple of minutes until the zest has softened. Remove zest and place in a bowl of cold water.
- Add apricots and peaches to the hot syrup, simmer gently for 4–5 minutes, turning the fruit until just tender, but not too soft. Allow fruit to cool in the syrup.
- Peel and thinly slice the oranges.
- To make salad, arrange orange slices decoratively on a platter. Top with well-drained apricots and peaches, pour over the passionfruit pulp and garnish with orange zest.

Serve with low-fat ice-cream, low-fat yoghurt or low-fat fruit sorbet.

Orange, Cucumber and Mint Salad

SERVES 4-6

dressing
$^1/_2$ cup cider vinegar
2 tablespoons finely chopped mint
freshly ground black pepper

4 navel oranges, peeled and cut into thin rounds
2 large apple cucumbers, peeled and cut into thin rounds
1 cup finely chopped spring onions

- To make dressing, place all ingredients in a glass jar and shake well.
- To make salad, combine all ingredients and add dressing. Toss lightly and serve.

Serve with fish, turkey or chicken.

Orange, Mango and Mint Salad with Balsamic Vinaigrette

SERVES 4–6

A citrusy mango delight that is given a little kick along by the watercress.

2 tablespoons Balsamic Vinaigrette (page 128)
1 large bunch watercress
3 navel oranges, peeled and segmented
1 ruby red grapefruit, peeled and segmented
2 mangoes, peeled and diced
1 salad onion, peeled and diced
1 cup mint leaves
1 tablespoon finely chopped chives

- Make the dressing as instructed and set aside.
- Prepare watercress as for salad greens.
- To make salad, combine all ingredients in a large bowl, toss lightly and serve.

Serve with chicken, fish, prawns, calamari or lamb.

Pasta, Mushroom and Peanut Salad with Honey, Soy and Sesame Dressing

SERVES 4–6

$1/4$ cup Honey, Soy and Sesame Dressing (page 135)
500 g pasta (ribbon or spiral)
500 g mushrooms
1 cup chopped spring onions
1 cup chopped dry-roasted peanuts
$1/2$ cup finely chopped parsley

- Make the dressing as instructed and set aside.
- Cook pasta in plenty of boiling water until *al dente*. Drain and refresh under cold water. Drain well.
- Chargrill mushrooms.
- To make salad, combine all ingredients while pasta and mushrooms are still warm. Add the dressing, toss lightly and serve.

Serve with chargrilled vegetables, chicken, fish, lamb or beef.

Pasta, Pumpkin and Pea Salad

SERVES 4–6

An ideal salad for vegetarians. You can serve it as a side salad with your choice of meat. For a variation, substitute sweet potato for the pumpkin. Dry-roasting the pumpkin or sweet potato and the seeds or nuts before using will give the finished salad a rich nuttiness.

dressing

1 × 200 ml tub honey-flavoured low-fat vanilla yoghurt
2 tablespoons coconut milk (page 2)
1 teaspoon cumin
1 teaspoon vindaloo curry paste (page 11)
1 teaspoon finely chopped fresh ginger

500 g pasta (ribbon or spiral)
500 g pumpkin, peeled and cubed
2 cups fresh or frozen peas
1/4 cup sunflower seeds or sesame seeds or chopped cashews
1/2 cup finely chopped chives

- To make dressing, combine all ingredients in a small bowl and whisk together until smooth and creamy.
- Cook pasta in plenty of boiling water until *al dente*. Drain and refresh under cold water. Drain well.
- Cook pumpkin and peas until just tender. Drain well.
- To make salad, combine cooked pasta, pumpkin, peas and dressing in a salad bowl and toss lightly. Scatter over the seeds or nuts and chives and serve immediately.

Serve with chicken, fish, lamb or beef.

Pawpaw, Mango and Pineapple Salad with Orange Mustard Dressing

SERVES 4–6

Pawpaw is low in kilojoules, high in fibre and rich in vitamins A and C, making it a highly regarded health food. When buying, look for firm unblemished skin, a vibrant yellow-orange colour and a sweet aroma.

dressing
$1/2$ cup freshly squeezed orange juice
2 tablespoons white wine vinegar
$1/4$ teaspoon hot English mustard
1–2 teaspoons grainy mustard
1 tablespoon finely chopped chives

1 butter lettuce
1 large pawpaw, peeled, seeded and sliced into thin wedges
3 mangoes, peeled and sliced
1 cup chopped fresh pineapple
$1/4$ cup finely chopped basil
2 tablespoons finely chopped mint

- To make dressing, place all ingredients in a jar and shake well.
- Prepare lettuce as for salad greens.
- To make salad, combine all ingredients in a large bowl, toss lightly and serve.

Serve with chicken, fish, turkey, prawns or chargrilled vegetables.

Peach and Nectarine Salad with Balsamic Vinaigrette

SERVES 4–6

The sweet juicy flesh of the peach soaks up the balsamic dressing to make a perfect summer salad. Serve this with warm cooked meats.

dressing
2 tablespoons Balsamic Vinaigrette (page 128)
2 teaspoons finely grated orange zest

500 g peaches, halved and stoned
500 g nectarines, halved and stoned
1 cup freshly squeezed orange juice
2 tablespoons mint leaves

- Make the dressing as instructed, adding the orange zest. Set aside.
- Preheat the oven to 180°C.
- Place peaches and nectarines, cut side up, in a baking dish. Pour over orange juice and bake until fruits are soft and beginning to brown. Remove from the oven. Spoon over any juices at the bottom of the dish and place under a hot grill to brown the tops further.
- Place grilled fruits on a platter. Spoon over the dressing and garnish with mint leaves.

Serve with chargrilled vegetables, fish, chicken, turkey, beef or lamb.

Pear, Apple and Sultana Fruit Salad

SERVES 4–6

This salad is best served cold with warm custard on cool winter evenings.

sweet syrup
zest of 1 lemon
2 cups Sweet Cinnamon Syrup (page 147)

500 g pears, cored and quartered
500 g Granny Smith apples, cored and quartered
1 cup sultanas
$1/4$ cup brandy

- Wash lemon and, using a citrus zester, remove long strips of zest. If you don't have a zester you can remove the peel with a sharp knife or vegetable peeler, being careful not to remove too much of the pith. Cut the peel into long thin strips.
- Make the sweet syrup as instructed and add zest to hot syrup. Cook, stirring continuously for a couple of minutes, until the zest has softened. Remove zest and place in a bowl of cold water.
- Add pears and apples to the hot syrup, simmer gently for 4–5 minutes, turning fruit until just tender but not too soft. Remove from heat, add sultanas, and allow fruits to cool in the syrup.
- Remove fruits from syrup and set aside. Add brandy to the syrup, bring to the boil and reduce a little. Cool before spooning over the cooled fruit. Garnish with lemon zest.

Serve with warm custard, low-fat ice-cream, low-fat yoghurt or low-fat fruit sorbet.

Pears and Plum Berry Fruit Salad

SERVES 4–6

The soft, buttery flesh of the pears soaks up the flavour and colour of the syrup, making it delicious to the eye and mouth. It is an ideal autumn fruit salad. If you can't locate fresh raspberries and blueberries, substitute thawed frozen berries.

sweet syrup
2 cups Sweet Berry Syrup (page 147)
zest of 1 orange

400 g pears, cored and quartered
400 g blood plums, stoned and quartered
200 g raspberries
100 g blueberries

- Make the sweet syrup as instructed and set aside.
- Wash orange and, using a citrus zester, remove long strips of zest. If you don't have a zester you can remove the peel with a sharp knife or vegetable peeler, being careful not to remove too much of the pith. Cut peel into long thin strips.
- Blanch zest in boiling water for a couple of minutes until it has softened. Remove zest and place in a bowl of cold water.
- Add pears and plums to the hot syrup, simmer gently for 4–5 minutes, turning fruit until just tender but not too soft. Remove from heat and allow fruits to cool in the syrup. (The longer the fruits are allowed to stand, the stronger the colour.) Add berries just prior to serving and garnish with orange zest.

Serve with warm custard, low-fat ice-cream, low-fat yoghurt or low-fat fruit sorbet.

Julie Stafford's Salads

Potato Salad with Mustard Mayo Dressing

SERVES 4–6

This salad is best made with the very smallest baby potatoes you can find. They are sweeter and make a fabulous-looking salad.

1/2 cup Mustard Mayo Dressing (page 138)
2 kg new baby potatoes
herbs (e.g. mint, chives, dill)

- Make the dressing as instructed and set aside.
- Wash potatoes and, if necessary, use a small scrubbing brush to remove all dirt. Plunge into boiling water and cook until they are just tender. (If you cook potatoes in water that is boiling too rapidly, the skins tend to split.)
- To make salad, combine warm potatoes with dressing and garnish with herbs. Toss lightly and serve.

Serve with chargrilled vegetables, fish, chicken, turkey, beef, lamb and Tomato, Onion and Basil Salad (page 115) or Beetroot and Spinach Salad with Raspberry Vinegar (page 33).

Prawn, Asparagus and Mango Salad

SERVES 4–6

When making a salad using seafood, use only the freshest you can find. Fresh seafood should smell like the sea!

dressing
1/4 cup apple juice concentrate
2 teaspoons finely chopped fresh ginger
1 cup freshly squeezed orange juice
3/4 cup dry sherry
1 tablespoon low-salt soy sauce
1 tablespoon finely grated orange zest
1–2 tablespoons cornflour
2 tablespoons water

600–800 g raw prawns, shelled, deveined and tails removed
1 cup white wine or fish stock
500 g asparagus, sliced diagonally and blanched
200 g baby spinach leaves, chopped and blanched
1 mango, peeled and cubed
4 spring onions, sliced diagonally
1/4 cup coriander leaves

- To make dressing, combine all ingredients, except cornflour and water, in a saucepan and bring to the boil. Combine cornflour and water to make a paste, add to the ingredients in the saucepan and stir, cooking just long enough to slightly thicken. Allow to cool.
- Using a sharp knife, make a split down the underside of the prawns. Place wine or stock in a shallow pan or wok and bring to the boil. Add the prawns and toss quickly until they turn pink and remove. Plunge into chilled water or fish stock.

Julie Stafford's Salads

- To make salad, combine all ingredients except the coriander. Toss lightly and turn out onto a large salad platter. Spoon over the dressing and garnish with coriander.

Serve with chargrilled vegetables, rice or potatoes.

Radicchio with Balsamic Vinegar and Chives

SERVES 4–6

The rich, red colour and strong, sharp flavours of the radicchio are tempered by the mellow balsamic vinegar. A very dramatic-looking salad!

dressing
$1/4$ cup balsamic vinegar
1–2 tablespoons finely chopped chives
freshly ground black pepper

1–2 large heads radicchio

- Remove outer radicchio leaves and discard. Cut in half, remove core and break off leaves. Wash and dry thoroughly as for salad greens.
- To make salad, combine lettuce and dressing, toss lightly and serve.

Serve with chargrilled vegetables, fish, chicken, turkey, beef, lamb, Potato Salad with Mustard Mayo Dressing (page 87) or Roasted Sweet Potato and Rosemary Salad (page 95).

Red Cabbage, Capsicum and Redcurrant Salad

SERVES 4–6

Ideal for brightening up your barbecue table!

dressing
$2/3$ cup white wine vinegar
$1/3$ cup freshly squeezed lemon juice
4 tablespoons apple juice concentrate
a pinch of salt
a pinch of black pepper
1 tablespoon olive oil

1 firm red cabbage
3 red capsicums, seeded and cut into thin strips
200 g redcurrants
1–2 tablespoons finely chopped chives
freshly ground black pepper

- To make dressing, place all ingredients except the oil in a jar and shake well. Pour into a small bowl and slowly whisk in the oil.
- Remove outer cabbage leaves and core and discard. Shred remaining cabbage very finely, wash thoroughly and blanch.
- Blanch capsicum.
- Remove stems from the berries and discard. Wash berries.
- To make salad, combine all ingredients and add dressing. Toss lightly and serve.

Serve with chargrilled vegetables, chicken, turkey, beef or lamb.

Rice Salad with Chicken, Peas and Bean Sprouts

SERVES 4–6

Rice is one of those versatile foods you should always cook more than you need. Keep the leftovers in the refrigerator and you can turn out fast healthy salads by adding your favourite leftover cooked vegetables, meats or fish, lots of fresh herbs and a good dressing. Raw rice doubles in size when cooked, so for 4 cups of cooked rice you will need $1^1/2$–2 cups raw rice.

$3/4$ cup Chinese Dressing (page 129)
4 cups cold cooked rice
250 g cold cooked chicken, chopped (skin and fat removed)
2 cups cold cooked peas
$1/2$ red capsicum, seeded and diced
1 cup finely sliced spring onions
100 g bean sprouts
$1/2$ cup finely chopped coriander
2 teaspoons grated lemon zest
1 teaspoon finely chopped red chilli

- Make the dressing as instructed and set aside.
- To make salad, combine all ingredients in a large bowl and add dressing. Toss lightly and serve.

Serve with Salad of Greens (page 97) or chargrilled vegetables.

Rice Salad with Fruits and Nuts

SERVES 4–6

*Use either brown or white rice for this recipe. Brown rice has
more fibre and nutritional value, but high-fibre ingredients such
as apples and dried fruits will help to boost the overall fibre
content of a finished dish that is made with white rice.*

dressing
1 tablespoon lemon juice

3 tablespoons cider vinegar

a pinch of salt

$1/2$–1 teaspoon vindaloo curry paste (page 11) or sweet chilli sauce
(page 10)

3 tablespoons safflower oil

4 cups cold cooked rice

2 red apples (Fuji, Jonathan, Lady William), cored and cubed

1 cup finely chopped spring onions

1 cup raisins

$1/2$ cup chopped apricots

$1/2$ cup currants

$1/2$ cup cashews

$1/4$ cup chopped brazil nuts

$1/4$ cup chopped almonds

2 tablespoons finely chopped mint

- To make dressing, place all ingredients except the oil in a
  jar and shake well. Pour into a small bowl and slowly
  whisk in the oil.
- To make salad, combine all ingredients in a large bowl and
  add dressing. Toss lightly and serve.

Serve with Salad of Greens (page 97), chargrilled vegetables or
fish.

Roasted Roma Tomato and Thyme Salad

SERVES 4–6

Ripe, firm Roma (also called Italian or plum) tomatoes are the only ones to use for this salad – they have great flavour and hold their shape when cooked. Allow them to cool to room temperature for the flavours to mature before serving.

dressing

1 tablespoon balsamic vinegar

a pinch of salt

freshly ground black pepper

2 tablespoons olive oil

12–14 Roma tomatoes, halved

1 tablespoon chopped thyme

extra thyme leaves

- To make dressing, place all ingredients except the oil in a jar and shake well. Pour into a small bowl and slowly whisk in the oil.
- Preheat oven to 150°C.
- Place tomatoes on a lined baking tray. Scatter over chopped thyme. Roast for 20–40 minutes or until tomatoes are soft and brown around the edges.
- To make salad, remove tomatoes carefully onto a platter and spoon over the dressing. Scatter more thyme leaves over the top. Allow the tomatoes to cool to room temperature and serve.

variation

For Roasted Roma Tomato and Thyme Salad with Egg, make salad as instructed. Hard-boil 6 eggs, shell and remove egg yolks. Chop up the egg whites and scatter over the top of the salad before serving.

Serve with Salad of Greens (page 97), beef, lamb, chicken, fish or chargrilled vegetables.

Roasted Sweet Potato and Rosemary Salad

SERVES 4–6

Sweet potatoes are an excellent source of dietary fibre and contain more nutrients than the white potato. However they come together well in this salad for taste and colour. I tend to keep the skins on when making this dish to maximise the valuable nutrients and dietary fibre.

dressing
1 tablespoon balsamic vinegar
a pinch of salt or cayenne pepper
2 tablespoons olive oil

1.5 kg pontiac potatoes, washed and cubed
1.5 kg sweet potatoes, washed and cubed
1 tablespoon olive oil
$1/4$ cup chopped rosemary
freshly ground black pepper
2 tablespoons finely chopped chives

- To make dressing, place all ingredients except the oil in a jar and shake well. Pour into a small bowl and slowly whisk in the oil.
- Preheat the oven to 180°C.
- Toss potatoes in oil, rosemary and pepper. Spread them on a non-stick baking tray and bake in the oven until lightly browned and tender.
- To make salad, place cooked potatoes on a platter, pour over dressing while potatoes are still warm, and garnish with chives.

Serve with Salad of Greens (page 97), beef, lamb, chicken, fish or chargrilled vegetables.

Salad Niçoise

SERVES 4-6

A popular Mediterranean salad, preferably made with fresh tuna and the very best olives. You can substitute well-drained canned tuna in seawater. As a variation, try substituting baby spinach leaves for lettuce – they give this classic salad a whole new dimension.

2 tablespoons Italian Vinaigrette (page 136) or Mustard Vinaigrette (page 138)

800 g–1 kg fresh tuna steaks or 2 × 425 g cans tuna, well drained

4 hard-boiled eggs

1 lettuce, washed and roughly chopped

3 Roma tomatoes, peeled, seeded and chopped

100 g green beans, topped, tailed, cut in four and blanched

100 g yellow beans, topped, tailed, cut in four and blanched

$1/2$ red capsicum, seeded and chopped

$1/2$ yellow capsicum, seeded and chopped

1 red onion, peeled and thinly sliced

10 black olives

$1/2$ cup Italian parsley leaves

- Make the dressing as instructed and set aside.
- Chargrill or steam tuna until just cooked and still a little pink inside. Set aside and keep warm. If using canned tuna, drain and break up into bite-sized pieces.
- Shell eggs, cut in half and discard the yolks. Chop the remaining egg whites.
- To make salad, place lettuce in the bottom of a salad bowl. Add egg whites and all other ingredients except the parsley. Break up the cooked tuna with a fork and add to the salad bowl. Add dressing. Scatter parsley over the top and toss lightly just before serving.

This salad is best served as a meal on its own.

Salad of Greens

There is literally no end to the variety of lettuces and greens available to make the classic green salad – radicchio, red butter, green and red oakleaf, cos (romaine), red perilla, baby bok choy, spinach, collard, red and green mustard, sorrel, red and green chard, witlof (Belgian endive), curly endive, chicory, cress, watercress, red beet greens, kale and so on. You'll find some or most of them at your local greengrocer's, the supermarket and speciality shops. Most salad greens can be grown easily and cheaply in your own garden, in pots or even a window box.

With all the variety around, rarely would you bother making a green salad today using only one type of lettuce. Salad leaves have such wonderful flavours and most complement each other; they may be delicate, assertive, buttery, mustardy, peppery, tart, lemony or nutty. They come in all shades of green and reddish-purple colours; the leaves may be feathery, curly, crinkly, soft or frilled. And best of all, they all look so good together in the salad bowl.

If you choose fresh vibrant greens that display little discolouration or wilting, they only need to be washed thoroughly and dried well before use. If you need to store them, do so in a perforated plastic bag and place in the crisper section of your refrigerator. It is important to wash the leaves in lots of cold water to remove the sand and grit that tend to get caught in the foliage grooves. Be gentle, as the leaves bruise easily. Dry the washed leaves in a salad spinner, between paper towels or wrap loosely in a tea towel. If you follow these guidelines, you will find that a good combination of the freshest greens hardly needs to be dressed – simply add handfuls of fresh herbs such as chives, basil, coriander, parsley, mint, oregano or thyme (or a combination). Grated lemon or orange zest or seeds such as poppyseeds and sesame seeds and chopped nuts also add plenty of flavour.

If you dress the salad, use the absolute minimum of dressing and toss through just before serving. If you are using an oil-based dressing, the leaves should be very dry so the oil coats the leaves. You'll find plenty of dressing ideas on pages 128–146.

If you haven't tried all these beautiful leaves, make this the year to bring greens back to your table. Any combination can be tossed together to form the basis of a fast, healthy meal. They are loaded with vitamins A and C, and are high in iron, calcium and potassium. Best of all, they are a very low-kilojoule food.

While there are no set rules for the quantity of greens to serve per person, I would allow approximately 50 g per diner.

Salad of Warm Baby Carrots with Orange, Honey and Sesame Dressing

SERVES 4-6

A perfect salad to add colour and sweetness to a main meal. Carrots are high in vitamins C and A, so this is nutritious as well as delicious.

dressing
$1/2$ cup freshly squeezed orange juice
1 teaspoon finely chopped fresh ginger
1 teaspoon sweet chilli sauce (page 10)
2 tablespoons honey
1 teaspoon lime juice
1 tablespoon finely chopped parsley
2 teaspoons sesame oil (optional)
1 teaspoon sesame seeds

600-800 g baby carrots

- To make dressing, place all ingredients except the oil in a jar and shake well. Pour into a small bowl and slowly whisk in the oil.
- Cut tops off carrots, leaving about 2 cm of green stem on each. Scrub carrots to remove any dirt, and blanch.
- To make salad, add dressing to warm carrots, toss lightly, and stand for at least an hour before serving.

Serve with beef, lamb, chicken, fish, turkey, boiled potatoes, beetroot or Salad of Greens (page 97).

Snow Pea, Mango and Avocado Salad with Pesto Dressing

SERVES 4–6

The crispiness of the snow pea is matched by the soft creamy texture of the mango and avocado.

dressing
2 tablespoons Vinaigrette (page 146)
1 teaspoon pesto (page 8)

300 g snow peas, topped and tailed
2 mangoes, peeled and cubed
2 firm avocados, peeled, stoned and cubed
$1/2$ cup basil leaves
$1/4$ cup finely chopped spring onions

- Make the dressing as instructed, adding the pesto. Set aside.
- To make salad, combine all ingredients, toss lightly and serve.

Serve with Salad of Greens (page 97), beef, lamb, chicken, fish or chargrilled vegetables.

Spicy Chargrilled Mushroom Salad

SERVES 4–6

So little work for so much warm pleasure!

dressing
2 tablespoons olive oil
1–2 teaspoons vindaloo curry paste (page 11)
1 teaspoon finely chopped red chilli
1 teaspoon finely chopped fresh ginger

1 kg cultivated mushrooms

- Wipe mushroom tops and remove stems. Place mushrooms in a bowl.
- Combine dressing ingredients and pour over mushroom. Toss to coat well.
- Chargrill mushrooms in batches on a chargrill pan or under a griller until they begin to brown. Save any juices at the bottom of the cooking pan.
- Pile cooked mushrooms on a salad platter and spoon over any cooking juices.

Serve with chargrilled vegetables, beef, lamb, chicken, turkey or fish.

Spicy Oriental Meatball and Tomato Salsa Salad

SERVES 4–6

When buying minced beef always buy premium or diet mince as it has the least fat. If you cannot find lean mince, buy fillet steak, remove all fat and mince it in a food processor.

dressing
1/2 cup Spicy Oriental Dressing (page 142)

peanut oil

meatballs
1 kg lean beef mince
2 egg whites
1/4 cup pinenuts
1 teaspoon cumin
1 tablespoon finely chopped mint

300 g mixed lettuce leaves
500 g Roma tomatoes, diced or 500 g cherry tomatoes, halved
1/2 cucumber, peeled and diced
1/2 cup chopped mint leaves

- Make the dressing as instructed and set aside.
- To make the meatballs, first wipe the base of a non-stick frying pan with peanut oil and heat. Place all ingredients in a bowl and mix well. Shape into small balls and place evenly around the base of the hot pan. Cook the meatballs on both sides until browned and cooked through. Remove from the pan, reserve the cooking juices, and keep meatballs warm.

- To make salad, wash and dry lettuce and scatter it over the base of a platter or bowl. Combine tomato, cucumber, mint and dressing, and spoon the mixture over the lettuce. Add the warm meatballs, cooking juices, toss lightly and serve.

Serve with baked potatoes or crusty bread.

Spicy Sprouts Salad

SERVES 4-6

Who could ever have imagined that so much goodness could be packed into such a nondescript food? Sprouts may not be much to look at, but are nutty, crunchy and a good source of vitamin C and iron.

dressing
$^1/_2$ cup freshly squeezed orange juice
1 teaspoon lime juice
$^1/_2$ teaspoon cumin
$^1/_4$ teaspoon five-spice powder (page 4)

1 cup sultanas
150 g mung bean sprouts
150 g lentil sprouts

- To make dressing, place all ingredients in a glass jar and shake well.
- To make salad, combine all ingredients and add dressing. Toss lightly and serve.

Serve with baked potato, chargrilled vegetables, chicken, fish, beef or lamb.

Springtime Vegetable Salad

SERVES 4–6

Nothing tastes quite like young, baby-sized vegetables picked fresh from the garden in springtime.

$^1/_2$ cup Herb French Dressing (page 134)
12 new baby potatoes, washed thoroughly
1 bunch asparagus spears (choose the very thin ones)
200 g snow peas or sugar peas, topped and tailed
200 g yellow beans, topped, tailed and cut in half
12 baby yellow squash, topped and tailed
1 red capsicum, seeded and cut into strips
12 baby carrots
1 small cauliflower, broken into florets
1 small head broccoli, broken into florets
herbs (e.g. basil, mint, coriander leaves)
freshly ground black pepper

- Make the dressing as instructed and set aside.
- Cook the potatoes in water until just tender, and drain well. While still warm, place them in a bowl with the dressing and set aside.
- Blanch asparagus, snow peas or sugar peas and beans together. Drain well and add to potatoes.
- Blanch squash, capsicum and carrots together. Drain well and add to potatoes.
- Blanch cauliflower and broccoli together. Drain well and add to potatoes.
- To make salad, add your herbs of choice and pepper to taste to the potatoes. Toss lightly, and allow to stand for at least 1 hour before serving.

Serve with Salad of Greens (page 97), fish, beef, chicken or lamb.

Stone Fruit Salad

SERVES 4–6

If only stone fruit were available all year around . . . what a wonderful world it would be! All four fruits used in this recipe have quite unique flavours, and need very little fussing with.

sweet syrup
1 cup Sweet Syrup (page 146)
1 teaspoon finely grated lemon zest
1 teaspoon finely grated orange zest
1 tablespoon Grand Marnier, Cointreau or Galliano

200 g peaches, stoned and quartered
200 g nectarines, stoned and quartered
200 g apricots, stoned and quartered
200 g stoned cherries

- Make the sweet syrup as instructed, adding zest and liqueur. Set aside.
- Combine fruits in a salad bowl in decorative layers, pour over slightly cooled syrup and serve.

Serve with low-fat ice-cream, low-fat yoghurt or low-fat fruit sorbet.

Summer Berry Fruit Salad

SERVES 4–6

This way of serving berries brings out their absolute best. The berry season is so very short, so find as many ways as possible to serve these delicate, delicious fruits, fresh from the bush, shrub or vine, while they are in season.

sweet syrup
1 cup Sweet Cinnamon Syrup (page 147)
$1/4$ cup brandy

300 g strawberries, washed and hulled
200 g raspberries
100 g blueberries
200 g boysenberries
50 g redcurrants

- Make the sweet syrup as instructed, adding the brandy. Set aside and allow to cool.
- Combine berries in a bowl, pour over the cooled syrup and serve.

Serve with low-fat ice-cream, low-fat yoghurt or low-fat fruit sorbet.

Sweet Potato and Chickpea Salad with Chilli Tahini Dressing

SERVES 4–6

Use the red-skinned, orange-fleshed sweet potato for this recipe. It is rich in vitamins C and E, and high in dietary fibre.

dressing

200 ml low-fat yoghurt
2 tablespoons tahini (page 10)
1 tablespoon honey
2 tablespoons lemon juice
2–3 teaspoons sweet chilli sauce (page 10)
2 tablespoons finely chopped red capsicum

2 large sweet potatoes, peeled and cubed
100 g green beans, topped, tailed and cut into 2 cm lengths
4 cups cooked chickpeas
1 avocado, peeled and cubed
2 sticks celery, finely chopped
1 tablespoon capers

- To make dressing, place all ingredients in a glass jar and shake well.
- Cook sweet potatoes in water until just tender and drain well.
- Blanch beans.
- To make salad, combine all ingredients except the capers in a large bowl and add dressing. Toss lightly, garnish with capers and serve.

Serve with Salad of Greens (page 97), red radicchio or curly endive.

Swordfish and Radicchio with Red Pepper Mayo Dressing

SERVES 4–6

The Red Pepper Mayo is also fabulous over prawns and lobster.

$3/4$ cup Red Pepper Mayo (page 141)
1 cup stock (chicken, fish, vegetable) or $1/2$ cup white wine plus
    $1/2$ cup water
1 tablespoon olive oil
$1/2$ lemon, sliced
4 bay leaves
1 small shallot, peeled and sliced
800 g swordfish, cut into small even-sized pieces
1 large head radicchio
1 red onion, peeled and sliced thinly
fresh basil leaves (garnish)

- Make the dressing as instructed and set aside.
- Combine stock, oil, lemon, bay leaves and shallot in a pan. Bring the liquid to a gentle simmer. Add fish, cover and allow the steam to slowly cook the fish. Turn the fish carefully so that it cooks on both sides. When the fish is nearly cooked, turn off the heat, leave the pan covered, and allow the fish to cool in the cooking liquid. (You may prefer to chargrill the fish for this recipe.)
- Discard the outer leaves from the radicchio, cut into quarters and tear leaves from the core and prepare leaves as for salad greens.
- To make salad, combine radicchio, onion, basil and drained fish (in that order). Add dressing and toss lightly, taking care not to break the fish, and serve.

Serve with chargrilled vegetable or Roasted Roma Tomato and Thyme Salad (page 94).

Tabbouleh Rice Salad

SERVES 4–6

Tabbouleh is traditionally made with cracked wheat, but rice is an ideal substitute, especially for people with wheat allergies.

2 tablespoons Garlic Vinaigrette (page 133) or $^1/_4$ cup Vinaigrette
   (page 146)
2 cups cold cooked brown rice
4 tomatoes, peeled, seeded and diced
4 spring onions, finely chopped
1 cup chopped parsley
1 cup chopped coriander
$^1/_2$ cup mint leaves
freshly ground black pepper

- Make the dressing as instructed and set aside.
- To make salad, combine all ingredients, add dressing, and pepper to taste. Toss lightly and serve.

Serve with chargrilled vegetables, fish, chicken, turkey, beef, lamb, potatoes, Salad of Greens (page 97) or baked potato.

Tandoori Chicken Salad

SERVES 4–6

A spicy, Indian-influenced chicken salad.

dressing
2 tablespoons balsamic vinegar
1 teaspoon freshly squeezed lemon juice

600–750 g chicken fillets, skin and fat removed
1 cup low-fat yoghurt
$1/4$ cup tandoori paste (page 11)
100 g torn lettuce leaves, washed thoroughly
4 Roma tomatoes, chopped
1 cucumber, peeled, halved, seeded and sliced
$1/4$ cup mint leaves

- Place chicken in a shallow baking dish.
- Combine the yoghurt and tandoori paste, pour over chicken and cover with foil. Marinate for at least 1 hour.
- Preheat the oven to 200°C.
- Bake the chicken, covered, for 1 hour. Remove the foil for the last 10 minutes and allow the chicken to cool before slicing thinly. Strain the cooking juices, reserving 1 tablespoon.
- Alternatively, remove the chicken from the marinade and grill or barbecue. (If grilling or barbecuing, you will need to bring marinade to the boil in a saucepan and strain before adding to the dressing.)
- To make dressing, combine vinegar, lemon juice and reserved strained cooking juices, and mix well.
- To make salad, combine lettuce, tomato, cucumber, mint, dressing and toss lightly. Place salad in the centre of a platter, top with chicken and serve.

Serve with chargrilled vegetables or potatoes.

Tandoori Lamb Salad

SERVES 4-6

A warm and fruity way to serve lamb.

dressing
1 tablespoon olive oil
1 tablespoon freshly squeezed lemon juice

600–750 g lean lamb fillets
1 cup low-fat yoghurt for marinade, extra to serve
$1/4$ cup tandoori paste (page 11)
2 red apples, cored and chopped finely
1 cucumber, peeled, halved, seeded and sliced
1 cup sultanas
2 oranges, peeled and chopped finely
$1/4$ cup mint leaves

- Place lamb in a shallow baking dish.
- Combine the yoghurt and tandoori paste, pour over the lamb and cover with foil. Marinate for at least 1 hour.
- Remove lamb from marinade and chargrill for 5–7 minutes, turning once or until the lamb is done to your liking. Allow lamb to rest before slicing thinly. Alternatively, the lamb can be cut into very thin strips and threaded onto meat skewers. Chargrill or barbecue the lamb and remove from skewers before serving.
- Bring marinade to the boil, strain and reserve 1 tablespoon.
- To make dressing combine oil, lemon juice and the reserved strained cooking juices.
- To make salad, combine apple, cucumber, sultanas, oranges, mint, dressing and toss lightly. Arrange lamb on a platter with the salad to one side. Serve with extra yoghurt.

Serve with chargrilled vegetables or Salad of Greens (page 97).

Three Bean and Vegetable Salad

SERVES 4–6

This is an oldie but a goodie, which is easily adapted by changing the combination of vegetables or the dressing.

2 tablespoons Vinaigrette (page 146)
4 cups mixed, well-drained, cooked beans (red kidney, garbanzo, butter beans, green lima beans, Great Northern Beans)*
2 tomatoes, seeded and diced
1 green capsicum, seeded and diced
1 red capsicum, seeded and diced
1 red onion, peeled and diced
1 tablespoon capers
$^1/_2$ cup finely chopped parsley

* If using beans in a can, drain well and rinse off excess salt by running the beans under cold water in a sieve and drain again. If using dried beans, check the pack for cooking instructions. Beans generally need to be soaked overnight, covered with fresh water and cooked gently for a couple of hours until tender.

- Make the dressing as instructed and set aside.
- To make salad, combine all ingredients and add dressing. Toss lightly and serve.

Serve with chargrilled vegetables, potatoes, Salad of Greens (page 97) or radicchio.

Tomato and Mushroom Pasta Salad with Red Pepper Mayo Dressing

SERVES 4-6

Pasta is a high-carbohydrate food that provides plenty of fibre and energy. This nutritious meal makes an ideal lunch or snack.

3/4 cup Red Pepper Mayo (page 141)
500 g pasta (e.g. spaghetti, spiral noodles, ribbon pasta, penne)
500 g Roma tomatoes, quartered, seeded and cut into strips
a pinch of salt
freshly ground black pepper
200 g snow peas, topped, tailed and halved lengthwise
400 g mushrooms, wiped clean
1 red onion, peeled and cut into thin wedges
1/2 cup chopped basil
extra basil leaves
grated parmesan cheese (optional)

- Make the dressing as instructed and set aside.
- Cook pasta until *al dente*, drain, run under cold water to refresh and drain well.
- While pasta is cooking, place tomatoes in a bowl with salt and pepper and allow to stand.
- Blanch snow peas.
- Chargrill mushrooms on both sides and cut in half.
- To make salad, combine all ingredients except the basil and cheese, add half the dressing and toss lightly. Turn out salad into a clean bowl or onto a salad platter and spoon over remaining dressing. Garnish with basil leaves and freshly grated parmesan cheese if using.

Serve with Salad of Greens (page 97) or radicchio.

Tomato, Onion and Basil Salad

SERVES 4–6

This salad must be made with only the best tomatoes. Ripe Roma tomatoes are excellent. Big, red, juicy hydroponic tomatoes or home-grown Grosse Lisses are also ideal.

dressing
$1/2$ cup malt vinegar
a pinch of salt
freshly ground black pepper
1 tablespoon finely chopped parsley

6 large tomatoes, washed and sliced into rounds
4 medium white salad onions, peeled and sliced into thin rounds
$1/2$ cup basil leaves
extra basil leaves

- To make dressing, place all ingredients in a glass jar and shake well.
- To make salad, place alternate layers of tomato, onion and basil in a bowl, finishing with a layer of tomatoes. Add dressing and allow to stand for at least an hour before serving.
- Garnish with basil leaves.

Serve with chargrilled vegetables, fish, chicken, turkey, beef, lamb, potatoes, Salad of Greens (page 97), radicchio or Witlof and Cucumber Salad (page 126).

Tropical Chicken, Cashew and Sultana Salad

SERVES 4–6

This is a favourite salad, boasting lots of complementary flavours and crunchy nuts, chewy sultanas and the bright warm colours of mango, pawpaw and banana. The cashews can be added raw or dry-roasted to give a much stronger nutty flavour.

$1/2$ cup Orange Curry Dressing (page 139)
2 tablespoons dried basil leaves
freshly ground black pepper
800 g–1 kg chicken fillets, skin and fat removed
2–3 bananas, peeled and sliced
1 tablespoon lemon juice
2 mangoes, peeled and chopped
$1/2$ pawpaw, peeled, seeded and chopped
1 cup chopped cashews
1 cup sultanas
$1/4$ cup coriander leaves

- Make the dressing as instructed and set aside.
- Combine basil and pepper and rub into chicken. Allow to stand for at least 2 hours. Chargrill chicken on both sides until well browned. Slice chicken while still warm. Set aside and keep warm.
- Toss bananas in lemon juice.
- To make salad, combine all ingredients except coriander in a salad bowl. Add dressing, toss lightly and allow to stand for at least an hour. Garnish with coriander just before serving.

Serve with chargrilled vegetables, Salad of Greens (page 97) or baby spinach leaves.

Tuna and Ribbon Pasta Salad

SERVES 4–6

Freshly cooked tuna steaks are exceptional, but you can't go past the value of having a few cans of tuna in brine sitting on your pantry shelves for those moments when you can't get fresh fish and you need a meal in a hurry.

400 g ribbon pasta
1 × 425 g can tuna, well drained
juice of $1/2$ lemon
1 red onion, peeled and diced
$1/2$ green capsicum, seeded and diced
$1/2$ red capsicum, seeded and diced
100 g cherry tomatoes, halved
2 tablespoons chopped dill
2 tablespoons chopped basil
freshly ground black pepper

- Cook pasta until *al dente*. Drain, run under cold water and drain well.
- To make salad, combine all ingredients in the order listed, add pepper to taste, toss lightly and serve.

Serve with chargrilled vegetables, Salad of Greens (page 97), radicchio or Witlof and Cucumber Salad (page 126).

Vegetable Combo Salad with Curry Coconut Dressing

SERVES 4-6

Choose your favourite vegetables when making this dish, and try to get in a wide variety for their nutritional value, colour and texture. The oil in the dressing is not really necessary (substitute 2 tablespoons water instead), but the flavour of the spices is enhanced by its use.

dressing
2 teaspoons olive oil
$1/2$ onion, peeled and diced
1 teaspoon crushed garlic
1 teaspoon finely chopped fresh ginger
1 teaspoon turmeric
1 teaspoon coriander
1 teaspoon garam masala
1 teaspoon cumin
1 tablespoon cornflour
$1/2$ cup coconut milk (page 2)
1 cup low-fat milk or soymilk

1 kg mixed vegetables: choose from broccoli, cauliflower (cut into florets), carrots, zucchini, squash (cut into chunks), capsicum (cut into strips), Brussels sprouts (halved), celery, green beans (cut diagonally), snow peas, sugar peas (topped and tailed), mushrooms (halved)
chopped coriander leaves

- To make the dressing, place the oil, onion, garlic, ginger and spices in a small pan and gently cook for about 2 minutes. Mix cornflour with a little of the coconut milk to make a paste, add remaining combined milks, pour into

the pan, and stir continuously until it thickens. Leave to cool.
- Blanch vegetables.
- To make salad, combine all vegetables, add dressing, coriander, and serve.

Serve with fish, chicken, turkey, beef, lamb, rice or Salad of Greens (page 97).

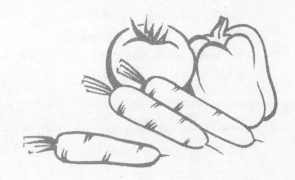

Vegetable Rice Salad

SERVES 4-6

This is a quick-and-easy salad to make, especially if you have leftover cooked rice in the refrigerator. Use the vegetable suggestions here as a guideline and vary the salad by using what is available and suits your taste.

2–4 tablespoons Ginger Vinaigrette (page 134) or Hot Vinaigrette
   (page 136)
4 egg whites, lightly beaten
1 red capsicum, seeded and diced
1 yellow capsicum, seeded and diced
4 cups cold cooked rice
2 cups cold cooked peas
500 g cold cooked, peeled and cubed pumpkin
1 cup finely sliced spring onions

- Make the dressing as instructed and set aside.
- Cook egg whites in a lightly oiled non-stick frying pan until set. Remove from pan and chop.
- Blanch capsicums if desired.
- To make salad, combine all ingredients in a bowl. Add dressing and allow to stand for at least an hour before serving.

Serve with chargrilled vegetables, fish, chicken, turkey, beef, lamb, potatoes or Salad of Greens (page 97).

Waldorf Salad

If an apple a day keeps the doctor away, then this classic salad is an investment in good health. It is a great-tasting salad, too.

1 cup Cucumber Dressing (page 130)
3 Granny Smith apples, cored and diced
3 red apples (Jonathan, Fuji, Lady William or Red Delicious), cored and diced
2 sticks celery, finely chopped
$^{1}/_{2}$ cup walnuts, chopped

- Make the dressing as instructed and set aside.
- To make salad, combine all ingredients in a bowl. Pour over dressing and allow to stand for at least an hour before serving.

Serve with chargrilled vegetables, fish, chicken, turkey, beef, lamb, potatoes, Salad of Greens (page 97), radicchio or Witlof and Cucumber Salad (page 126).

Warm Chicken, Coconut and Chilli Salad

SERVES 4–6

One benefit of a multicultural society is the marriage of many food ideas and ingredients to create a style of food not particularly common to any one culture, but uniquely Australian.

dressing

1 × 200 ml tub honey-flavoured low-fat vanilla yoghurt

2 teaspoons low-fat, cholesterol-free commercial mayonnaise

1 tablespoon pickled ginger (page 4)

1 tablespoon coconut milk (page 2)

1–2 teaspoons sweet chilli sauce (page 11)

1 teaspoon finely chopped red chilli

1 teaspoon finely chopped coriander

1 butter lettuce or 200 g baby spinach leaves

800 g–1 kg skinless chicken fillets

1 red capsicum, seeded, diced and blanched

1 yellow capsicum, seeded, diced and blanched

1 tablespoon chopped coriander

- To make dressing, place all ingredients in a small bowl and whisk together until smooth and creamy.
- Remove core from butter lettuce and prepare leaves as for salad greens, or wash spinach leaves and drain well.
- Chargrill or steam chicken until cooked. Slice thinly. Set aside and keep warm.
- To make salad, arrange butter lettuce or spinach on individual plates. Combine dressing, capsicums and chicken in a bowl and toss lightly, and divide equally between individual plates. Spoon over any remaining dressing and garnish with coriander.

This salad is best served on its own or with cooked rice.

Watercress, Orange and Olive Salad with a Tangy Lemon Dressing

SERVES 4–6

This simple salad relies on the happy marriage of peppery watercress, buttery lettuce, salty olives and sweet orange. They are flavoured with just a little oil, lemon juice and some chives, to add that little bit of sharpness.

dressing
2 tablespoons freshly squeezed lemon juice
a pinch of salt
a pinch of black pepper or cayenne pepper
1 tablespoon olive oil

1 small head butter lettuce
1 large bunch watercress
6 navel oranges
$3/4$ cup black olives
$1/4$ cup finely chopped chives

- To make dressing, place all ingredients except the oil in a jar and shake well. Pour into a small bowl and slowly whisk in the oil.
- Remove core from butter lettuce and prepare leaves as for salad greens.
- Prepare watercress as for salad greens.
- Peel oranges, cut in half lengthwise and slice into thin rounds.
- The olives can be left whole or halved and pitted.
- To make salad, combine all ingredients and add dressing. Toss lightly and serve.

Serve with fish, chicken or turkey.

Winter Fruit Salad

SERVES 4–6

A salad that combines the textures of dried and fresh fruits, creating a medley of sensational flavours. It can be prepared ahead of time and kept in the refrigerator.

sweet syrup
zest of 1 lemon
zest of 1 orange
1 cup Sweet Cinnamon Syrup (page 147)
1 cup freshly squeezed orange juice
$1/2$ cup muscat, brandy or port

100 g dried apricots
100 g dried pears, cut into strips
100 g dried nectarines
100 g dried figs
100 g sultanas
200 g pears, cored and quartered
200 g Granny Smith apples, cored and quartered
100 g slivered almonds

- Wash lemon and orange and, using a citrus zester, remove long strips of zest. If you don't have a zester you can remove peel with a sharp knife or vegetable peeler, being careful not to remove too much of the pith. Cut the peel into long thin strips.
- Make the sweet syrup as instructed, adding orange juice and muscat, brandy or port. Add zest to hot syrup and cook, stirring continuously, for a couple of minutes until the zest has softened. Remove zest and place in a bowl of cold water.
- Add dried fruits, pears and apples to the hot syrup, and simmer gently for 4–5 minutes, turning fruit, until just

tender but not too soft. Allow fruits to cool in the syrup.
Add almonds and garnish with zest prior to serving.

Serve with warm custard, low-fat ice-cream, low-fat yoghurt
or low-fat fruit sorbet.

Witlof and Cucumber Salad with Dill Vinegar

SERVES 4–6

The sharp taste of the witlof (Belgian endive) is cut by the bland flavour of the cucumber, and the herb vinegar brings out the best in both. A perfect salad to serve with cold meats.

dressing
$1/2$ cup Dill Vinegar (page 131)
1 tablespoon finely chopped shallots
1 teaspoon finely chopped dill

300 g witlof (Belgian endive), chopped roughly
500 g peeled, seeded and chopped white cucumber flesh (use apple, Lebanese or European)
freshly ground black pepper

- Make the dressing as instructed, adding shallots and dill. Set aside.
- To make salad, combine all ingredients and add dressing and pepper to taste. Toss lightly and serve.

Serve with cold meats, especially lamb and chicken, slices of fresh tomato, boiled potatoes, grated raw beetroot or Salad of Warm Baby Carrots with Orange, Honey and Sesame Dressing (page 99).

I offer here a selection of traditional-style **dressings and** a few variations. In many cases, my aim is to cut back on the fat content or to provide a more nutritional fat content or, in some cases, to cut out the fat completely. Quite often a squeeze of lemon juice, a little red or white wine vinegar or just the right herb or combination of herbs is a dressing in itself, and focuses attention on the flavour of the quality fresh ingredients instead of the dressing. I've also included recipes for **sweet syrups,** which can be poured over warm or cold fruits to add flavour, or used to cook fruits.

Avocado Dressing (oil free)

MAKES 1 CUP

1 ripe avocado
1–2 tablespoons freshly squeezed lemon juice
200 ml low-fat yoghurt
2 teaspoons sweet chilli sauce (more if you like it hot, page 10)
1 tablespoon finely chopped chives
a pinch of salt or cayenne pepper

Blend all ingredients together until smooth and creamy. Keep sealed and refrigerated. This dressing can be thinned with dry white wine or apple juice.

Balsamic Vinaigrette

MAKES 1/3 CUP

4 tablespoons balsamic vinegar
1–2 cloves garlic, peeled and bruised
2 tablespoons safflower or olive oil

Place all ingredients except the oil in a jar and shake well. Pour into a small bowl and slowly whisk in the oil. Keep sealed and refrigerated.

Chinese Dressing (oil free)

MAKES ³/₄ CUP

¹/₂ cup freshly squeezed orange juice
¹/₄ cup mirin
2 teaspoons fish sauce
1 teaspoon five-spice powder (page 4)
1 tablespoon apple juice concentrate
1 cm piece fresh ginger, peeled and finely chopped
2 tablespoons finely chopped spring onions

Combine all ingredients in a screw-top jar and shake well before using. Keep sealed and refrigerated.

Citrus Vinaigrette

MAKES ¹/₃ CUP

1 recipe Vinaigrette (page 146)
1–2 teaspoons freshly squeezed lemon juice
2 tablespoons freshly squeezed orange juice

Make the vinaigrette as instructed, adding the juices. Keep sealed and refrigerated.

Creamy Mayonnaise

MAKES ³/₄ CUP

200 ml low-fat yoghurt
1 tablespoon low-fat, cholesterol-free commercial mayonnaise (page 5)
1 tablespoon apple juice concentrate
1 teaspoon dry mustard
¹/₄ teaspoon black pepper

Combine all ingredients in a screw-top jar and shake well before using. Keep sealed and refrigerated.

Cucumber Dressing (oil free)

MAKES ³/₄ CUP

200 ml low-fat yoghurt
1 tablespoon low-fat, cholesterol-free commercial mayonnaise (page 5)
1 cucumber, peeled, seeded and grated
1 tablespoon freshly squeezed lemon juice
1 tablespoon cider vinegar
a pinch of paprika

Combine all ingredients in a screw-top jar and shake well before using. Keep sealed and refrigerated.

Dairy-free Mayonnaise (thin)

MAKES 1^{1}/$_{4}$ CUPS

1 cup low-fat soymilk
1 tablespoon lemon juice
2 teaspoons mustard
2 tablespoons apple juice concentrate
1 tablespoon finely chopped shallots or chives
a pinch of salt
1 tablespoon safflower oil

Place all ingredients except the oil in a jar and shake well.
Pour into a small bowl and slowly whisk in the oil. Keep
sealed and refrigerated.

Dill Vinegar

MAKES ^{1}/$_{2}$ CUP

^{1}/$_{2}$ cup white wine vinegar
a pinch of salt
a pinch of pepper
2 tablespoons finely chopped dill

Combine all ingredients in a screw-top jar and shake well
before using. Keep sealed and refrigerated.

French Dressing (oil free)

MAKES 1¹/₄ CUPS

²/₃ cup white wine vinegar
¹/₃ cup freshly squeezed lemon juice
4 tablespoons apple juice concentrate
a pinch of salt
a pinch of black pepper

Combine all ingredients in a screw-top jar and shake well
before using. Keep sealed and refrigerated.

Garlic French Dressing (oil free)

MAKES 1¹/₄ CUPS

1 recipe French Dressing (page 132)
1–4 cloves garlic, peeled and bruised

Combine all ingredients in a screw-top jar and shake well
before using. Keep sealed and refrigerated.

Note: The longer the dressing stands, the more intense the
garlic flavour. Chopped or crushed garlic gives an immediate
and intense garlic flavour.

Garlic Vinaigrette

MAKES ¹/₄ CUP

1 recipe Vinaigrette (page 146)
1–4 cloves garlic, peeled and bruised

Make the vinaigrette as instructed, adding the garlic. Note: The longer the vinaigrette stands the more intense the garlic flavour. Chopped or crushed garlic gives an immediate and intense garlic flavour.

Ginger French Dressing (oil free)

MAKES 1¹/₄ CUPS

1 recipe French Dressing (page 132)
1–2 cm piece fresh ginger, peeled and finely chopped or 1–2 teaspoons
    finely chopped, pickled ginger (well drained) (page 4)

Combine all ingredients in a screw-top jar and shake well before using. Keep sealed and refrigerated.

Ginger Vinaigrette

MAKES $1/2$ CUP

1 recipe Vinaigrette (page 146)
1 teaspoon freshly squeezed lemon juice
2 tablespoons freshly squeezed orange juice
2 teaspoons apple juice concentrate (optional)
1–2 cm piece fresh ginger, peeled and finely chopped or 1–2 teaspoons
    finely chopped pickled ginger (well drained) (page 4)

Make the vinaigrette as instructed, adding the juices, apple
juice concentrate and ginger.

Herb French Dressing (oil free)

MAKES $1^1/4$ CUPS

1 recipe French Dressing (page 132)
1–2 tablespoons finely chopped fresh herbs (coriander, basil, parsley,
    chives, mint)

Combine all ingredients in a screw-top jar and shake well
before using. Keep sealed and refrigerated.

Herb Vinaigrette

MAKES ¹/₂ CUP

1 recipe Vinaigrette (page 146)
1 teaspoon freshly squeezed lemon juice
2 tablespoons freshly squeezed orange juice
2 teaspoons apple juice concentrate (optional)
1–2 tablespoons finely chopped fresh herbs (coriander, basil, parsley, chives, mint)

Make the vinaigrette as instructed, adding juices, apple juice concentrate and fresh herbs.

Honey, Soy and Sesame Dressing

MAKES ¹/₂ CUP

2 tablespoons white wine vinegar
2 tablespoons low-salt soy sauce
2 tablespoons honey, warmed
1 tablespoon water
2 tablespoons sesame oil

Place all ingredients except the oil in a jar and shake well. Pour into a small bowl and slowly whisk in the oil. Keep sealed and refrigerated.

Hot Vinaigrette

MAKES ¹/₄ CUP

1 recipe Vinaigrette (page 146)
1–2 teaspoons seeded and finely chopped red chilli
1–2 teaspoons apple juice concentrate
¹/₄–¹/₂ teaspoon vindaloo curry paste (page 11)

Make the vinaigrette as instructed, adding chilli, apple juice concentrate and curry paste.

Italian Vinaigrette

MAKES ¹/₂ CUP

1 recipe Vinaigrette (page 146)
1–2 teaspoons freshly squeezed lemon juice
2 teaspoons apple juice concentrate
1 tablespoon finely chopped shallots
1 tablespoon peeled, seeded and finely chopped tomato
2 teaspoons finely chopped fresh oregano or parsley

Make the vinaigrette as instructed, adding lemon juice, apple juice concentrate, shallots, tomato and oregano.

Lemon Vinaigrette

MAKES $1/4$ CUP

1 recipe Vinaigrette (page 146)
1–2 teaspoons freshly squeezed lemon juice

Make the vinaigrette as instructed, adding lemon juice.

Mustard French Dressing (oil free)

MAKES $1^{1}/4$ CUPS

1 recipe French Dressing (page 132)
3 teaspoons grainy mustard
1 teaspoon finely grated orange zest

Combine all ingredients in a screw-top jar and shake well before using. Keep sealed and refrigerated.

Mustard Mayo Dressing (creamy)

MAKES ³/₄ CUP

200 ml low-fat yoghurt
1 tablespoon apple juice concentrate
1 tablespoon low-fat, cholesterol-free commercial mayonnaise (page 5)
2 tablespoons grainy mustard
1 tablespoon lemon juice

Combine all ingredients in a screw-top jar and shake well
before using. Keep sealed and refrigerated.

Mustard Vinaigrette

MAKES ¹/₃ CUP

1 recipe Vinaigrette (page 146)
1 teaspoon Dijon mustard
2 teaspoons grainy mustard
2 tablespoons freshly squeezed orange juice
2 teaspoons apple juice concentrate

Make the vinaigrette as instructed, adding mustard, juice and
apple juice concentrate.

Orange Chilli Dressing

MAKES 1 CUP

$^1/_2$ cup freshly squeezed orange juice

2 teaspoons finely chopped and seeded red chilli

1 teaspoon sweet chilli sauce (page 10)

2 tablespoons apple juice concentrate

1 teaspoon freshly squeezed lime or lemon juice

2 teaspoons peanut oil

Place all ingredients except the oil in a jar and shake well. Pour into a small bowl and slowly whisk in the oil. Keep sealed and refrigerated.

Orange Curry Dressing (oil free)

MAKES $^2/_3$ CUP

$^1/_2$ cup freshly squeezed orange juice

2 tablespoons cider vinegar

1–2 teaspoons curry powder or 1 teaspoon vindaloo curry paste (page 11)

$^1/_2$ teaspoon peeled and finely chopped fresh ginger

$^1/_2$ teaspoon sweet chilli sauce (page 10)

1 teaspoon honey

2 teaspoons finely chopped shallots

Combine all ingredients in a screw-top jar and shake well before using. Keep sealed and refrigerated.

Orange Mustard Dressing (oil free)

MAKES $2/3$ CUP

1/2 cup freshly squeezed orange juice
1/2 teaspoon hot English mustard
1–2 teaspoons grainy mustard
2 tablespoons white wine vinegar
1 tablespoon finely chopped chives

Combine all ingredients in a screw-top jar and shake well
before using. Keep sealed and refrigerated.

Raspberry Vinegar (oil free)

MAKES 1 CUP

100 g fresh raspberries
1/3 cup red wine vinegar
2 tablespoons apple juice concentrate

Place all ingredients in a small saucepan. Bring to the boil,
simmer for 2–3 minutes and cool. Pour into bottles and seal.
Once opened, the vinegar should be kept in the refrigerator.

Red Pepper Mayo

MAKES ³/₄ CUP

1 red capsicum, halved and seeded
1 tablespoon low-fat, cholesterol-free commercial mayonnaise (page 5)
2 teaspoons sweet chilli sauce (page 10)
200 ml plain low-fat yoghurt
a pinch of black pepper
1 tablespoon finely chopped chives

To make the dressing, first blanch capsicum in water, stock or white wine (or a combination of all three). When the capsicum is cold, chop roughly. Place capsicum and remaining dressing ingredients except the chives in a blender and blend until smooth. Add chives. Store in a jar in the refrigerator and shake well before using.

Spicy Oriental Dressing (oil free)

MAKES $^1/_2$ CUP

2 tablespoons freshly squeezed lime or lemon juice
1 teaspoon seeded and finely chopped red chilli or sweet chilli sauce
    (page 10)
3 tablespoons low-salt soy sauce
2 tablespoons apple juice concentrate
1 tablespoon fish sauce
1 clove garlic, crushed
1 cm piece fresh ginger, peeled and finely chopped or 1 teaspoon finely
    chopped pickled ginger (page 4)

Combine all ingredients in a screw-top jar, and shake well
before using. Keep sealed and refrigerated.

Sweet Chilli Dressing

MAKES 2 TABLESPOONS

1 teaspoon sweet chilli sauce (page 10)
2 teaspoons freshly squeezed lemon juice
2 teaspoons freshly squeezed orange juice
1 teaspoon cider vinegar
1 tablespoon safflower oil

Combine all ingredients, except oil, in a screw-top jar and
shake well. Slowly whisk in the oil. Keep sealed and
refrigerated.

Sweet Vinaigrette

MAKES $1/3$ CUP

1 recipe Vinaigrette (page 146)
1 teaspoon freshly squeezed lemon juice
1 teaspoon freshly squeezed orange juice
2 teaspoons apple juice concentrate

Make the vinaigrette as instructed, adding juices and apple juice concentrate.

Tahini Curry Dressing

MAKES $2/3$ CUP

$1/2$ cup freshly squeezed orange juice
1 teaspoon vindaloo curry paste (page 11)
2 tablespoons hulled tahini (page 10)
1 teaspoon apple juice concentrate
1 teaspoon freshly squeezed lemon juice
1–2 teaspoons finely chopped fresh coriander or mint (optional)

Mix a little orange juice with the curry paste before combining all ingredients in a screw-top jar. Shake well before using. Keep sealed and refrigerated.

Tangy Tahini Dressing

MAKES ²/₃ CUP

1 tablespoon honey
200 ml low-fat yoghurt
2 tablespoons hulled tahini (page 10)
1–2 tablespoons freshly squeezed lemon juice
1–2 cloves garlic, crushed

Warm honey before combining all ingredients in a screw-top jar. Shake well before using. Keep sealed and refrigerated.

Thai Dressing

MAKES ¹/₂ CUP

¹/₄ cup low-salt soy sauce
2 teaspoons finely chopped pickled ginger (page 4)
1 clove garlic, crushed
2 tablespoons rice wine vinegar
1 tablespoon finely chopped fresh coriander
1 tablespoon finely chopped fresh Thai mint
1 teaspoon sesame seeds
a pinch of salt or cayenne pepper
1 tablespoon sesame oil

Combine all ingredients, except oil, in a screw-top jar and shake well. Pour into a small bowl and slowly whisk in the oil. Keep sealed and refrigerated.

Tomato Dressing

MAKES ³/₄ CUP

1 × 170 ml can salt-free tomato juice
1 tablespoon low-fat, cholesterol-free commercial mayonnaise (page 5)
2 teaspoons dry mustard
a pinch of black pepper
1 teaspoon basil
1 tablespoon balsamic vinegar
1 tablespoon apple juice concentrate
1 tablespoon finely chopped fresh mint
1 tablespoon finely chopped fresh parsley

Combine all ingredients in a screw-top jar, and shake well before using. Keep sealed and refrigerated.

Vinaigrette

Vinaigrette ingredients can also be whisked together in the salad bowl you are going to use. Add salad ingredients and toss well to coat.

MAKES ¼ CUP

1 tablespoon white wine vinegar
a pinch of salt and freshly ground black pepper or substitute salt and
    pepper with a good pinch of cayenne pepper
4 tablespoons safflower or olive oil

Combine all ingredients, except oil, in a screw-top jar and shake well. Pour into a small bowl and slowly whisk in the oil. Keep sealed and refrigerated.

Sweet Syrup (basic)

MAKES 1 CUP

1 cup water, unsweetened fruit juice or sweet white wine
¼ cup apple juice concentrate
1 teaspoon freshly squeezed lemon juice
½ vanilla bean (optional)

Place all ingredients in a saucepan, stir and bring to the boil. Simmer for a few minutes and, if using vanilla bean, strain before using.

Sweet Berry Syrup

MAKES 1 CUP

1 cup water
1 cup unsweetened grape juice
$1/2$ cup blueberries
$1/2$ cup raspberries
1 tablespoon apple juice concentrate
2 teaspoons finely grated orange zest

Place all ingredients in a saucepan, stir and bring to the boil.
Simmer for a few minutes and strain syrup before using.

Sweet Cinnamon Syrup

MAKES 1 CUP

1 cup water or sweet white wine
$1/4$ cup apple juice concentrate
1 teaspoon freshly squeezed lemon juice
1 teaspoon ground cinnamon or $1/2$ cinnamon stick

Place all ingredients in a saucepan, stir and bring to the boil.
Simmer for a few minutes and strain syrup if using a cinnamon
stick. (A cinnamon stick gives a more subtle cinnamon
flavour.)

Sweet Ginger Syrup

MAKES 1 CUP

$^1/_2$ cup water
1 tablespoon apple juice concentrate
$^1/_2$ cup green ginger wine*
1 teaspoon finely grated lemon zest
1 teaspoon finely grated lime zest
1 teaspoon freshly squeezed lemon juice

* If you do not have green ginger wine, substitute 1 cm peeled fresh ginger or 1 tablespoon chopped glacé ginger and use 1 cup water.

Place all ingredients in a saucepan, stir and bring to the boil. Simmer for a few minutes and strain syrup if using fresh or glacé ginger.

Sweet Orange Marmalade Syrup

MAKES 1 CUP

$^1/_4$ cup water or lychee juice
$^3/_4$ cup freshly squeezed orange juice
2 tablespoons sugar-free marmalade
1 teaspoon finely grated orange zest

Place all ingredients in a saucepan, stir and bring to the boil. Simmer for a few minutes and strain syrup if necessary.

Index